SUICIDAL IDEATION

A BIBLICAL PERSPECTIVE FOR COUNSELORS

DANIEL R. BERGER II

ALETHIA
INTERNATIONAL
MINISTRIES

SUICIDAL IDEATION: A BIBLICAL PERSPECTIVE FOR COUNSELORS

Library of Congress Control Number: 2021901727
Trade Paperback ISBN: 978-0-9976077-3-4

Cover Artwork by: Priscilla and Elieser Loewenthal
Edited by: Gail Berger

Unless otherwise noted, all Scripture references in this book are taken from the *English Standard Version*, copyright © 2001 by Crossway, Inc. Used by permission. All rights reserved.

Published by Alethia International Publications
Taylors, SC

www.drdanielberger.com

Printed in the United States of America

To:

My teachers at CLCS,
with special thanks to
Brian Cameon
and
Mike Cumberledge.
Your lives faithfully
pointed me
to Jesus.

TABLE OF CONTENTS

ACKNOWLEDGMENTS

I want to thank God for His Word that provides us with all wisdom that is needed for life and godliness. I also want to thank my family for patiently allowing me to serve God through communicating His truths to others. I am grateful for several families who endured the loss of their own loved ones, taken the time to review this book, and to offer their feedback. As always, I wish to thank a group of wise counselors who have also read the initial manuscripts and influenced the final product of this book. Likewise, I am grateful to my editor, Gail Berger, for her work and sacrifice of time in effort to help minister to those in need.

DISCLAIMER

The material contained in this book is the result of years of counseling experience, research, and professional interviews, but it is not intended in any way to be taken as medical advice. Rather, the views and material expressed in this book are philosophical, theological, scientific, historical, and written in order to provide God's wisdom that will enable parents, counselors, educators, pastors, therapists, physicians, and other helpers to have biblical discernment and to be better equipped to offer genuine truth, love, and hope to those in their care.

OTHER BOOKS BY DR. BERGER

Mental Illness: The Necessity for Faith and Authority

Mental Illness: The Reality of the Spiritual Nature

Mental Illness: The Reality of the Physical Nature

Mental Illness: The Influence of Nurture

Mental Illness: The Necessity for Dependence

Rethinking Depression: Not a Sickness Not a Sin

Saving Abnormal: The Disorder of Psychiatric Genetics

Teaching a Child to Pay Attention: Proverbs 4:20-27

The Chemical Imbalance Delusion

The Insanity of Madness: Defining Mental Illness

The Truth About ADHD

ABBREVIATIONS

APA   The American Psychiatric Association

BMJ   *The British Medical Journal*

FDA   Federal Drug Administration

JAMA   *The Journal of the American Medical Association*

NAMI   The National Alliance on Mental Illness

NEJM   *The New England Journal of Medicine*

SI   Suicidal Ideation

WPA   World Psychiatric Association

ENDORSEMENTS

"With wonderful insight and clarity, Daniel Berger explores the difficult and ever-increasing problem of suicide. He first presents the unsuccessful secular attempts at understanding and solving the problem, and then having done that, he describes the biblical perspectives on the causes of suicide and the biblical method of preventing and resolving the problem. This book will be very helpful preventively for the individual contemplating suicide and for the counselor, friend, or family member who lives with or knows a person who is struggling with suicidal ideations." *- Dr Wayne Mack, ACBC Academy member, ACBC Africa Director, Former chair of the Biblical Counseling Department at The Master's University and Seminary, Founder and Professor of Biblical Counseling at Strengthening Ministries Training Institute*

"*Suicidal Ideation: A Biblical Perspective* sheds the radiant light of truth on a topic that for so long has been shrouded by a hopeless darkness. Dr. Berger meticulously walks the reader through the research, which reveals suicidal ideation not to be a problem of the body but of the soul; one that should be treated not by a psychological model but by a spiritual one. As a nurse who regularly works with patients struggling with suicidal ideations, I found Dr. Berger's research to be both eye-opening and empowering. I have repeatedly seen the failure of the psychological model to treat suicidal ideation and prevent attempts. There is a joy in knowing that Scripture not only addresses suicidal ideation, but also that the Bible provides instruction to those seeking to enter into the battle against it." - **Katie Piazza, Emergency Department RN/ Author of** *Victorious: A Mother and Daughter's Journey through the Valley of the Shadow*

"As a pastor who has counseled for over 22 years, I can honestly say that counseling those contemplating suicide as well as comforting those left behind after a suicide has taken place can be some of the most difficult and complex counseling circumstances. Dr. Berger offers a unique biblical counseling resource in that he uses secular material to expose how damaging a secular approach towards suicidal ideation can be while at the same time highlighting the immense hope that the Gospel of Jesus Christ offers to someone contemplating suicide. Regardless of experience, this book is a must read for all counselors, pastors, and people-helpers who desire to step into one of life's darkest situations." - **Ben Marshall, D.Ed.Min , Counseling Pastor at Canyon Hills Community Church, ACBC Fellow, Board Chairman of The Damascus House, author of** *Help! My Teen Struggles with Same-Sex Attraction,* **and contributing author to** *Men Counseling Men.*

"Suicidal ideation includes tremendous hopelessness and despair. Counselors and friends who care deeply long for insight into how to bring wise help. Dr. Daniel Berger provides such wisdom by showing the importance of discovering what people believe about their circumstances and who they are as people. Having this insight, the helper can support them to know the hope and life of Christ in their deep sorrow, experiencing him as the only genuine anchor of their soul." - **Anne Dryburgh, Ph.D., is an IABC and ACBC certified biblical counselor and a CABC (Commissioned Addictions Biblical Counselor). She is a long-time missionary in Belgium, Coordinator for *Reigning Grace Institute* Europe, and European team of *Truth in Love Biblical Counseling*. She is also on the advisory board of *Biblical Counselling Africa* and the *Fallen Soldiers March*, coordinator of the *European Biblical Counseling Network*, and author of *Debilitated and Diminished: Help for Women in Emotionally Abusive Marriages* and *(Un)ashamed: Christ's Transforming Hope for Rape Victims*.**

"Suicide is considered one of the fastest growing social phenomena of our time, leaving us with difficult questions that demand sensible, truthful, and wise answers that really get to the core of the problem and that offer real hope to those struggling with suicidal ideations. These answers are what Dr. Daniel Berger offers us in his excellent book, *Suicidal Ideations*. Through an interdisciplinary dialogue, he not only answers the difficult questions, but he also takes us to the heart of the problem—pointing toward the wise and sure direction of the Holy Scriptures, which all who care for those in despair must utilize if they are to offer genuine hope." - **Airton Williams, Pastor of the Christian Church of Reformed Confession, President of the Society for Interdisciplinary Bible Studies (SEBI University) and Pure Life Ministries Brazil, Historian, Certified Biblical Counselor (CEABI-Brazil), and author.**

"Dr. Berger has written a book that will flip your cultural understanding of suicide. Cultural norms recognize the seriousness of suicidal ideations, yet cannot offer the perspective that the truth of God's Word provides to a suffering soul. Dr. Berger provides helpers with the rationale behind the true origins of suicide along with practical biblical principles to help the hurting person to address the heart of suicidal thoughts in a manner that ultimately brings glory to God." - **Mark E. Shaw, author of** *The Heart of Addiction*, **founder of The Addiction Connection**

INTRODUCTION

I will never forget the first time that I personally helped a family to pick up the pieces of life after a completed suicide attempt. In this particular case, I did not know the man, who had been a faithful husband and a loving father. So, I was unaware that he had been struggling with suicidal ideations. Still, I wondered then how I would have tried to help him and how his completion would have affected me had I been counseling him or close to him.

After the suicide occurred, my wife and I were asked to share with this man's wife and daughters the terrible news and to help the family through this tragic experience. We remember vividly how we struggled to find both words of comfort and a legitimate explanation to offer. Yet, we both realized at that time that we needed to better understand this human phenomenon we call *suicide*, since we knew that one of the most common questions, which regularly haunts almost all people who remain after someone's suicidal completion, would be asked of us: "Why?" In truth, my wife and I were asking ourselves why anyone would willfully choose to end his/her own life?

Since that day, I have been tasked with the grievous privilege of helping individuals and families through similar circumstances. Whether it is attempting to help people struggling with suicidal ideation (thinking), those who recently attempted suicide, or the countless families whose loved ones had completed suicides, the question of "why" only intensified with each occurrence. Understanding why someone would choose to take his or her own life is an important pursuit and a necessary discussion if the number of attempted suicides is to be reduced and those struggling are to be helped.

I will also never forget the time several years ago when I began speaking regularly in various churches on the topic of depression from a biblical worldview/phenomenology. After one of the plenary sessions, I sat across the dinner table from a well-known and respected pastor of a local church. It was there that the pastor shared with me that he himself was contemplating suicide and that understanding his deeply sorrowful condition from a biblical vantagepoint had been positively life-changing for him. I had not even spoken on suicide that day. But by God's grace, that under-shepherd, while he still struggles with sorrow, has established a sure anchor for his soul that allows him to endure the fallen nature of this world and the many painful relationships and circumstances that God ordains all of us to experience in our lives.

But not every attempt to help people overcome suicidal ideation ends in joy and celebration. Sadly, I have also observed the opposite result and witnessed people choosing to act upon their suicidal thoughts after I, along with many others, have for hours prayed over and talked with those contemplating suicide. We are simply not afforded the responsibility or privilege of choosing another's choices, though we earnestly desire and make every effort to help them. This reality is true despite a counselor's faith or techniques. In fact, it is estimated that approximately

> 50% of psychiatrists and approximately 20% of
>
> other mental health professionals experience
>
> the loss of one or more patients to suicide over
>
> the course of their career.[1]

When anyone chooses to help others in areas of human depravity and fragility, especially in periods of overwhelming crisis and despair, that helper will surely experience both times of great encouragement and times of profound pain.

Over the years, I have observed a pattern in people who struggle with suicidal ideation, and the current trends in world news and the global increase of suicidal ideation

---

[1] Laurie Martin, "Demand for Suicide Prevention Increases," *Psychiatric Times Online* (September 16, 2020): https://www. psychiatrictimes.com/view/demand-for-suicide-prevention- increases?utm_source=sfmc%E2%80%8B&utm_medium=email %E2%80%8B&utm_campaign=09252020_PT_JAN-20-PSD0031_ TRC_Spravato%E2%80%8B%E2%80%8B&eKey=31158D64-F01A- 4DEA-AC1A-D3CE843FC9BC.

have further verified these elements. More importantly, this pattern is consistently explained throughout the Bible with often detailed accounts to consider. Hence, this book seeks to offer a clear understanding of the nature of suicidal ideation and a subsequent biblical approach to helping those in need.

A GROWING CONCERN

Suicidal attempts and completions are not merely heard about on the news these days; they are also directly impacting our own homes, our churches, and our communities. It is estimated that around 800,000 people complete suicide attempts each year,[2] which is a figure that does not include the even more staggering numbers of failed attempts.[3] With the increase in suicides trending

---

[2] Mareike Dreier, Julia Ludwig, Martin Härter, Olaf von dem Knesebeck, Johanna Baumgardt, Thomas Bock, Jorg Dirmaier, Alison J Kennedy, Susan A Brumby, and Sarah Liebherz, "Development and evaluation of e-mental health interventions to reduce stigmatization of suicidality - a study protocol," *BMC Psychiatry* vol. 19 (1): (May 17, 2019): 152; doi: 10.1186/s12 888-019-2137-0. PMID: 31101103; PMCID: PMC6525463.

[3] Maria A. Oquendo and Enrique Baca-Garcia, "Suicidal behavior disorder as a diagnostic entity in the DSM-5 classification system: advantages outweigh limitations," *World Psychiatry: official journal of the World Psychiatric Association (WPA)* vol. 13 (2) (2014): 128-30. doi:10.1002/wps.20116.

upward at an "alarming rate,"[4] the topic of someone contemplating whether or not to take his/her own life, though difficult to discuss, is more needed today than ever. Moreover, the vast majority of American citizens believe that discussing suicide prevention should be a national priority.[5]

But I want to make it clear from the outset of this book that simply bringing awareness to others of the need of suicidal prevention to a discussion is by itself not helpful. Instead, we need to talk about these issues from a biblical and empirical perspective that can provide understanding and deliverance before there is ever a crisis. What must be firmly established is genuine hope, which alone can rescue those in despair and those who have established deceitful and destructive ways of thinking.

THE NEED TO DISCERN

Although it is helpful to determine why someone would consider taking his/her own life, this understanding is not always easy to identify. "Ideations," which is a term often

---

[4] Deborah Brauser, "US Suicides Increasing at 'Alarming Rate," Says CDC," *Medscape Psychiatry* (June 7, 2018): https://www.medscape.com/viewarticle/897804.

[5] Laurie Martin, "Demand for Suicide Prevention Increases."

utilized to express ways of thinking or ideas, rest in a person's spiritual heart/mind. It is also in the spiritual/metaphysical mind that we find root motives and purposes which propel us to think, feel, and behave in either morally positive or morally destructive ways. But discerning what motives and ideas rest in a person's soul/mind is difficult and requires both spiritual discernment and the mutual establishment of a caring and trustworthy relationship(s).

Because the metaphysical soul is simply not accessible using scientific tools or applying the scientific method, a person's thoughts, desires, underlying motives, and life history—issues that help to answer the "why" question—must be "drawn out." Proverbs 20:5 explains,

> The purpose in a man's heart is like deep water,
>
> but a man of understanding will draw it out.

Both the *King James* and *New King James* Versions of the Bible translate this verse as:

> Counsel in the heart of man *is like* deep water;
>
> but a man of understanding will draw it out.

Before counsel can be given from one heart to another and replace destructive ways of thinking, the bad counsel or "ideation" in the troubled soul must be discerned. The thoughts or counsel in a person's heart—including purposes and ideas that would lead him/her to consider and attempt suicide—are difficult to extract but vitally important to understand and address.

To better understand suicidal ideation and to potentially resolve it, we must discover through a person's words (Proverbs 18:4) what deceitful and destructive ideas he/she has accepted and offer a fresh source of living water that comes from the Word of God. When people verbalize the desire to end their lives, they are beginning to reveal their spiritual hearts. Though, as will be further addressed throughout this book, suicidal thinking is always the fruit of a deeper root issue rather than being the main problem.

Matthew 12:34b expresses that "out of the abundance of the heart the mouth speaks." When an individual states his/her heart's content to be violent toward him/herself or others, such thinking is antithetical to God's righteousness, which is a "fountain of life" (Proverbs 10:11). "Ideation"— a person's metaphysical/spiritual thoughts or ideas—is revealed in words and behaviors (Luke 6:45); thus, a person's words should be considered diligently and be taken seriously.

Just as a large body of water takes time to fill and become deep, so too, it most often takes time for both bad and good counsel to control the human heart. Putting off bad counsel/deep dark waters of suicidal thinking and replacing it with the living Word of God is most often a lengthy process that requires a firm commitment by all involved. There are certainly seasons of intense counsel and prayer over a person who is critically struggling with suicidal thoughts. But finding victory over any destructive desire that is motivating a person toward harmful behavior is a process of putting off/destroying strongholds and putting on/renewing the mind that requires a compassionate and Christ-centered relationship(s) over time (Ephesians 4:20-25ff.).

It cannot be overstated that accurately understanding the source of a person's suicidal thinking is key to discovering the solution and helping people to find restorative hope.

Not only are there many people who have battled through suicidal ideation and found life-altering hope, but there are also countless people who have survived suicide attempts, and many even travel the world explaining the destructive nature of their past thinking, while expressing deep remorse for even considering suicide in the first place. While it is beneficial to hear the testimony of suicide survivors and to consider the empirical evidence available, the wisdom of God contained in His Word perfectly explains human nature and answers the "why" question critical to addressing suicidal thinking. Likewise, the Bible offers discernment to counselors, which exposes and explains the motives of the heart. In accordance, I desire this book to offer God's wisdom and corresponding empirical evidence concerning suicidal ideation, attempts, and completions, which I hope and pray will continue to be beneficial in helping people struggling with suicidal thoughts to find genuine hope and deliverance from the deep dark waters of the human soul.

As our study will reveal, apart from the wisdom of Christ— the giver of life and the only source of pure satisfying water, all other wisdom leads to spiritual death. If hope for suicidal ideation is to be realized, it will only be found in establishing Christ as our genuine hope—the anchor of our souls and the true fountain of life.

CHAPTER 1

SUICIDE IS ON THE RISE

For the last several decades, the number of suicidal attempts and completions have continued to consistently rise. The currently preferred theories and practices in today's society, which are widely believed to be altruistic, medically and scientifically based, and claimed to help people, continue to fail in both explaining and reversing this discouraging trend. Secular psychiatrist Allan Tasman discusses the continued rise in suicidal completions:

> In spite of improved understanding of risk factors and increased vigilance for suicide risk among mental health and other medical practitioners and families of those at risk, the suicide rate in the US continues to go up. . . . Between 2006 and 2016 the overall US suicide rate went up from 10.97 to 13.26 per 100,000 people. Those numbers may seem small, but they reflect an increase of just over 20% in

these 10 years. And, the trend lines don't look
much different going back to 2000.[6]

While it might be uncomfortable to hear for some, the rise
in suicidal thinking and completions is largely due to the
current phenomenological approach to suicide that views
the mindsets and behavior as if they were primarily
medical conditions that must be understood and treated
from the secular doctrines of humanism,
materialism/reductionism, and bio-determinism. This
failed humanistic approach to suicide has inadvertently
encouraged more people than ever to consider suicide as
an opportunity of self-deliverance and self-actualization
rather than being preventative.

Humanistic thinking in particular, which dominates much
of today's society and upholds the medical model of the
soul/psyche, is largely responsible for the upward trend in
suicidal thinking, attempts, and completions. This secular
faith presents suicide as a dignified individual right, as
reflected in the *Humanist Manifesto II*, authored by men
such as psychologist B.F. Skinner and the former president
of Planned Parenthood Alan F. Guttmacher. This
perspective states that

---

[6] Allan Tasman, "The Wrong Way on a Long and Winding
Road: Suicide in the US," *Psychiatric Times* (February 20, 2018):
http://www.psychiatric times.com/couch-crisis/wrong-way-
long-and-winding-road-suicide-us.

to enhance freedom and dignity the individual
must experience a full range of civil liberties in
all societies . . . . It also includes a recognition of
an individual's right to die with dignity,
euthanasia, and the right to suicide.[7]

It is clear that this way of thinking or "ideation" about human life has not helped to diminish suicide, and it is well past time for society to reconsider human nature and human phenomena apart from humanistic faith. Moreover, if suicide is dignified, why would anyone seek to remedy it?

Thankfully, there is an alternative perspective/approach available, and unless the current failed system is objectively examined and replaced, then the discouraging trend of suicidal thinking and completions will continue to rise, and the question of "why" will continue to be incorrectly answered.

---

[7] Francis Crick, B.F. Skinner, and Thomas Greening, et. al., *Humanist Manifestos I and II* edited by Paul Kurtz (Buffalo, NY: Prometheus Books, 1973), 19.

CHAPTER 2

NOT A MEDICAL ISSUE

Before better discovering what suicidal ideation actually is and what leads to or causes such thinking, one must first consider what it is not and what corresponding approaches to this view need to be discarded. Such a study is necessary in order to answer the question of why some people arrive at a mental state of desiring to end life. Moreover, if the upward trend in the number of completed suicides is to be reversed, a perspective apart from both the current psychiatric system of phenomenology and the corresponding humanistic worldview must honestly be considered.

Despite the reality that much of society views suicide as a human phenomenon that is primarily a medical issue, it is largely understood from the available empirical data and the rapidly growing testimonies of groups of "psychiatric survivors" that suicidal ideation increases in accordance with the level of psychiatric/medical treatment one receives. While this is not always the case, it is generally true, especially when suicide attempts are premeditated and not impulsive choices.

In the past, the claim has dogmatically been made that the medical model of the soul/psyche/mind is an "empirically driven" field and that it is scientifically sound. But many prominent psychiatrists have begun to be more honest about the paradigm's failure to even understand the problem, much less to heal or significantly help people whom the diagnostic system classifies as disordered. Cambridge psychiatrist Caleb Gardner and Harvard anthropologist Arthur Kleinman state this certainty:

> Ironically, although these limitations [of "biologic treatments"] are widely recognized by experts in the field, the prevailing message to the public and the rest of medicine remains that the solution to psychological problems involves matching the "right" diagnosis with the "right" medication. Consequently, psychiatric diagnoses and medications proliferate under the banner of scientific medicine, though there is no comprehensive biologic understanding of either the causes or the treatments of psychiatric disorders.[8]

Sedatives and tranquilizers can certainly offer short-term chemical restraints that suppress thinking and

---

[8] Caleb Gardner and Arthur Kleinman, "Medicine and the Mind-The Consequences of Psychiatry's Identity Crisis," *New England Journal of Medicine* (October 31, 2019): https://doi.org/10.1056/nejmp1910603.

consciousness through their chemical properties. But within their drug action, these drugs cannot positively change the underlying struggles in the immaterial soul that ultimately drives suicidal thinking.

While exploring the reality that suicidal ideation is not primarily a medical condition, it is helpful to understand that the medical model of mental health—the "bio-psycho-social/neo-Kraepelinian model" that dominates American society today and is the primary approach applied by secularists in attempting to address suicidal thinking—largely began with two of the first psychiatrists, Franz Anton Mesmer and Benjamin Rush. While both men proposed alternative approaches to the biblical understanding of the soul and mental, emotional, and behavioral struggles, it would be Dr. Benjamin Rush's published teachings that would authoritatively redefine the metaphysical human soul as something allegedly scientific and medically approachable.[9]

Significant to the discussion on suicidal ideation is the reality that Dr. Rush developed his theory of a material soul and the subsequent medical model in attempt to explain and approach his own son's suicidal thinking and attempted completions. Professor and historian at Columbia University Stephen Fried remarks on how the

---

[9] Daniel R. Berger II, *Saving Abnormal: The Disorder of Psychiatric Genetics* (Taylors, SC: Alethia International Publications, 2020).

mental struggles of Rush's son John "inspired" Rush to pen his psychiatric theory of the soul/psyche, which became the first psychiatric textbook in history, *Medical Inquiries and Observations, Upon Diseases of the Mind*.[10] Former president of the American Psychiatric Association John Oldham comments on this important historical event:

> [His son's first attempted suicide] turned his interest onto the field of mental health and mental illness. He was widely regarded as a very revered expert and compassionate physician who really moved away from the early pre-colonial myths—demons and witchcraft—**to focus in on the medical nature of the brain and the mind, and to treat it as a part of the body that we needed to understand more about** [emphasis added].[11]

---

[10] Stephen Fried, *Rush: Revolution, Madness, and the Visionary Doctor who became a Founding Father* 1st edition (NY: Random House, 2018), 7.

[11] Drew Ramsey and John M. Oldham, "A Brief History of American Psychiatry: From a Founding Father to Dr. Anonymous," *Medscape Psychiatry* (November 7, 2019): https://www.medscape.com/viewarticle/917451?nlid=132561_424&src=WNL_mdplsfeat_191112_mscpedit_psyc&uac=264124BV&spon=12&impID=2164621&faf=1.

It was upon Rush's foundational teaching (including the constructs of alcoholism and race) that the German psychiatrist Emil Kraepelin constructed his psychiatric statistical approach to the soul and the metaphysical phenomena of human nature and experiences. This phenomenology, sustained through the *DSM-5* constructs, represents the most influential mental health system in the world today. It is within this belief system that physicians are taught to explain the "why" of suicidal thinking as primarily having a medical/biological cause.

Rush's materialistic beliefs of the soul still undergird the fields of "psychiatry, clinical psychology, and the medical model of addictions."[12] Current president of the American Psychiatric Association Dilip Jeste comments on this well-established secular view of the mind/soul/psyche and how it relates to the brain and within societal relationships:

> The reality, I think, is that there is no conflict.
> Ultimately, the mind is a function of the brain,
> and the mind operates within a society.
> Neuroscientists are also realizing the
> importance of psychosocial aspects, and there
> is a growing social neuroscience, looking at the
> neurobiology of things such as loneliness, social
> isolation, and wisdom. The effects of

---

[12] Fried, *Rush*, 7.

psychosocial interventions such as meditation and long-term cognitive-behavioral therapy on the brain are now indisputable. I like to say that psychosocial interventions are often more biological in their effects than the drugs![13]

Treating the mind as if it is simply a function of the brain or a product of bodily processes has been devastating to individuals and societies throughout history. Yet, through the persistent teaching of men like Rush and Kraepelin, this failed materialistic view of the metaphysical soul has become the accepted approach to impairing, destructive, and distressful human phenomena.

When the bio-psycho-social model (neo-Kraepelinian model) was introduced in the late 60s through the early 70s as the primary secular/humanistic approach to the soul/psyche in America, it initiated the trend of increased suicidal attempts and completions. Sadly, as psychiatrist Georgia Gaveras discusses, those who hold to this belief system are the most impacted by it: "Physicians die by suicide at twice the rate of any other profession, with

---

[13] Dilip V. Jeste, "On the State of Psychiatry," *Current Psychiatry* vol. *19 (12)* (December 19, 2020): 34-36; also available from: https://www.mdedge.com/psychiatry/article/ 232726 /dilip-v-jeste-md-state-psychiatry/page/0/2.

roughly one doctor dying every day."[14] Succinctly stated, the current mental health system with its medical approach to the soul is not minimizing or reducing suicide; it is actually worsening the problem.

PSYCHIATRIC CARE

Many controlled studies, which psychiatrists themselves have conducted, have revealed that the deeper a person who is struggling with suicidal ideation enters into psychiatric treatment, the greater his/her risk of a suicidal attempt and the potential for a completion. For example, one article published in the *Journal of Social Psychiatry and Psychiatric Epidemiology* concluded that

> the results of a study in this issue of the *Journal* cast further doubt on the appropriateness of suicide risk assessment when patients receive hospital-based psychiatric care. **They also raise the disturbing possibility that psychiatric care**

---

[14] Georgia Gaveras, "As Americans face the worst mental health crisis in two decades, the psychiatrists tasked with helping them are also burning out," *Business Insider* (January 12, 2021): https://www.businessinsider.com/worst-mental-health-crisis-last-two-decades-psychiatrists-burning-out-2021-1.

might, at least in part, cause suicide [emphasis added].[15]

Psychiatrists Matthew Large and Christopher Ryan proceeded to point out in the same journal entry a chilling correlation between the level of psychiatric care a person receives and the proportional rise in the percentages of attempted suicides:

> The study found that, compared to those who had no psychiatric treatment in the previous year and after adjustment for other risk factors: those who only received psychiatric medication had 5.8 times the risk of suicide; those with at most outpatient psychiatric treatment had 8.2 times the risk of suicide; non-admitted patients who had contact with emergency departments had 27.9 times the risk of suicide. And admitted patients had 44.3 times the risk of suicide. Particularly striking are the strength of the associations between emergency room treatment and suicide and between inpatient

---

[15] Matthew M. Large and Christopher J. Ryan, "Disturbing Findings about the Risk of Suicide and Psychiatric Hospitals," *Journal of Social Psychiatry and Psychiatric Epidemiology* vol. 49 (June 2014): 1353-55; DOI: 10.1007/s00127-014-0912-2.

treatment and suicide. The magnitude of risk rations of nearly 30 or more for whole groups of patients who have contact with hospital-based services exceed both the risk of suicide associated with major psychiatric disorders and the strength of clinical risk factors of suicide among hospitalized patients by about an order of magnitude.[16]

Professor and clinical psychiatrist Paul Minot concurs, relating how psychiatry's reductionistic approach has not helped lessen suicidal ideation but, conversely, has increased it:

With more people carrying psychiatric diagnoses and receiving treatment than we ever could have imagined, you would expect to see improved psychiatric health and decreased suicide. But the opposite has occurred. The percentage of Americans on psychiatric disability benefits more than doubled from 1987 to 2007. And from 1999 to 2016, in the

---

[16] Ibid.

midst of this Age of Prozac, the incidence of
suicide in America has increased by 30%.[17]

Remarkably, a growing constituency of psychiatrists are now acknowledging the damaging nature of psychiatric treatments and the horrific history of biological attempts to treat the metaphysical soul, as well as speaking out on the need to replace existing protocol. In late 2020, psychiatrist Sami Tamimi published a book and several corresponding articles in which he transparently warned of the dangers of his own profession:

> Beware: Mental health services may be bad for
> your mental health . . . . Psychiatry has a dark
> history that embroiled it with some of the worst
> human rights atrocities, including active
> collusion with the eugenics movement and then
> the Nazis, where it was psychiatrists who first
> built and operated gas chambers to eliminate
> lives they deemed were not worth living. We
> have a duty as psychiatrists not to brush over
> these inconvenient episodes, but to face them,
> understand them, and learn from them, so we
> never repeat those horrors. Whilst it hasn't

---

[17] Paul Minot, "About Me," *Straight Talk Psychiatry* (December 31, 2019): https://paulminotmd.com/about-me/.

sunk to those terrible levels of inhumanity since, psychiatric practice remains complicit in incarcerating people and policing the population, which makes clinical endeavours impossible to disentangle from host political regimes' approaches to regulation and authority.[18]

The statistics themselves, when objectively evaluated, reveal that the current medical model (the philosophical perspective of attempting to explain the soul as biologically caused and attempting to treat problems of the soul with biological mechanisms) is, at the least, failing to help those who are struggling. At worst, the materialistic approach to the struggling soul is furthering mental turmoil and negative thoughts in those who need help.

These revelations do not determine that today's physicians are purposely hurting people. Instead, they expose that the medical model of the soul (materialism/reductionism) is ineffective in delivering genuine hope and remedies for humanity's deepest struggles. It could be argued that most clinicians genuinely desire to help individuals overcome

---

[18] Sami Timimi, "Insane Medicine: How the Mental Health Industry Creates Damaging Treatment Traps and How you Can Escape Them," *Mad in America* (October 12, 2020): https://www.madinamerica.com/2020/10/insane-medicine-preface/.

suicidal thoughts. But the presuppositional beliefs about the human soul/psyche force them to focus primarily on de-escalation and control – most often with psychotropic drugs– of those in their care rather than to establish a positive and meaningful way forward in life.

Though there is no evidence that the body causes people to think in deceitful and destructive ways or to take one's own life, physical impairments, valid diseases, sleep deprivation, psychotropic drugs, and troubling experiences can expose and highlight the true content of a person's spiritual heart. In other words, biological or medical issues can influence what already exists in the spiritual heart. This aspect of human nature is especially true in areas where self-control is diminished. For example, insomnia and sleep deprivation are regularly correlated with both suicidal attempts[19] and with delusions and hallucinations.[20] When people are unable to obtain deep restorative sleep, their true thoughts, desires, fears, and emotions are more easily acted upon and more frequently observed by others. Insomnia does not make people

---

[19] Bernert, Rebecca A, and Thomas E Joiner, "Sleep disturbances and suicide risk: A review of the literature." *Neuropsychiatric disease and treatment* vol. 3 (6) (2007): 735-43; doi:10.2147/ndt.s1248.

[20] For further study, see Daniel R. Berger II, *Saving Abnormal: The Disorder of Psychiatric Genetics* (Taylors, SC: Alethia International Publications, 2020).

angry,[21] immoral, anxious, deceived, or hopeless. Instead, missing out on necessary and profound sleep, especially for a length of time, will highlight both the amoral weaknesses and moral wickedness of human nature that already exist in every person's soul.

When guilt, traumatic events, fear, bitterness, anxiety, despair, broken relationships, and other human phenomena of the soul and fallen world hinder sleep, a person's discernment and self-control are diminished, and the content of his/her mind is more easily revealed. Sleep deprivation does not cause human deceit and spiritual turmoil; it simply reveals it. The physical nature and areas of nurture (experiences and education) can and do influence a person's thoughts. But these influences are not the primary cause of the heart's struggle. To discover the foundational problems of suicidal ideation, it is vital to understand what occurred in Genesis 3 that brought about the weakness and wickedness—the deep dark waters—of human nature inherent in everyone.

---

[21] Megan Brooks, "Sleep Loss Unleashes Anger," *Medscape Psychiatry* (September 15, 2020): https://www.medscape.com /viewarticle/937414?nlid=137426_2051&src=WNL_mdplsnews_ 200918_mscpedit_psyc&uac= 264124BV&spon=12&impID= 2572773&faf=1.

PSYCHIATRIC DRUGS

Answering the question of why some people decide to commit suicide and understating why the medical model has increased suicidal attempts requires greater attention. Specifically, psychiatric drugs must be considered as relevant in this discussion—as representing a major factor in the rise of suicide rates.

Despite the popular belief and heavy marketing, suicide is not diminished or remedied by psychotropic drugs, electric shock therapy, or any other physical manipulation of or alteration to the body. Rather, the volume of empirical evidence continues to reveal that suicidal ideation regularly intensifies with the increase in psychiatric drug intake and other alleged treatments.

In the *International Review of Psychiatry*, for instance, Drs. David Healy and Graham Aldred report how the drastic rise in suicide attempts and completions are best explained by the parallel rise in psychiatric prescriptions:

> Investigative Medication Routine translates
> such findings into estimates of likely adverse
> outcomes and explains why apparently
> increasing consumption of antidepressants
> would not be expected to lead to increased
> national suicide rates. **From this data, we**

conclude that there is a clear signal that
suicides and suicidal acts may be linked to
antidepressant usage. It would seem likely that
explicit warnings and monitoring in the early
stages of treatment could greatly minimize
these hazards [emphasis added].[22]

The Federal Drug Administration (FDA) in the United States
requires the black box warning to be printed on all
"antidepressant" labels. This warning not only indicates
that the drug is known to be dangerous but also informs
the consumer that the drug is "known to cause suicidal
ideation." In 2020, a group of psychiatric researchers
independently reexamined the FDA's black box warning to
determine if it was a legitimate claim. After conducting
thorough double-blind studies, these researchers
published their conclusions in the journal *Frontiers in
Psychiatry*:

Based on the sum of this evidence, regulatory
warnings regarding antidepressant-linked
suicidality are clearly warranted. When a clear
body of evidence points to increased
treatment-linked risk, patients and healthcare

---

[22] David Healy and Graham Aldred, "Antidepressant Drug
Use and the Risk of Suicide," *International Review of Psychiatry*
vol. 17 (3) (June 2005): 163.

providers should be made aware of these risks. To suggest otherwise both breaches the ancient injunction of primum non *nocere* (first, do no harm) and is not aligned with the practice of evidence-based medicine [emphasis added].[23]

The toxicity and increase in suicidal ideation and violence that psychotropic drugs regularly produce has been known for decades. Likely the most significant medical condition induced by prescribed psychiatric drugs is referred to as *akathisia*—a troubling neurological condition produced by several classes of psychiatric drugs and described as an intense irritability, a physical "torture"/pain, and/or a hopeless panic. Numerous psychiatrists, including the influential Nancy C. Andreasen, share their own findings about akathisia in *The Journal of Neuropsychiatry and Clinical Neurosciences*:

> *Akathisia*, characterized by a state of subjective and motor restlessness, is a common and unpleasant side effect of antipsychotic medication. Case reports have described both suicidality and violence as being precipitated by

---

[23] Glen I. Spielmans, Tess Spence-Sing, and Peter Parry, edited by Michael P. Hengartner, Maurizio Pompili, and Sami Timimi, "Duty to Warn: Antidepressant Black Box Suicidality Warning is Empirically Justified," *Frontiers in Psychiatry* (February 13, 2020): https://doi.org/10.3389/fpsyt.2020.00018.

this distressing condition . . . . Studies examining

the dysphoric effects and behavioral toxicity of

antipsychotic medications have also supported

the notion that this group of medications may

produce adverse behavioral side effects . . . .

Reports and studies linking suicide and/or

akathisia to the use of selective serotonin

reuptake inhibitors (SSRIs) have also implicated

a relationship between akathisia and changes in

mood and behavior induced by psychotropic

medications. The fact that this association may

extend beyond antipsychotics to include SSRI

medications increases the clinical importance of

this phenomenon, given the wide use of SSRIs in

depression, anxiety, and obsessive-compulsive

disorder.[24]

To deny or to ignore the "common" negative effects of akathisia and suicidal ideation is both to deny empirical evidence and to potentially further others into harm.

---

[24] E. Cem Atbasoglu, Susan K. Schultz, and Nancy C. Andreasen, "the Relationship of Akathisia with Suicidality and Depersonalization among Patients with Schizophrenia," *The Journal of Neuropsychiatry and Clinical Neurosciences vol. 13 (3)* (August 1, 2001): 336; https://doi.org/10.1176/jnp.13.3.336.

The specific scientific reasons that drugs designated as "antidepressants" and "antipsychotics" regularly increase suicidal ideation is that their chemical actions are mostly antagonists. This simply means that the drugs work by attacking healthy functions of the nervous system, which diminishes a person's control over his/her own natural mental and emotional processes and can agitate the consumer. Both the intoxication and unbearable "torture" the drugs produce are common complaints expressed by people under the drugs' influence and during withdrawal.

If the state of intense irritability and restlessness produced by ongoing consumption or the cessation after long-term use of these powerful drugs is not resolved, then panic and desperation often follow. Coupled with the suppression of desires, feelings, and discernment, which antidepressants and antipsychotics' drug actions both produce, a person intoxicated by these prescribed drugs can easily begin to see little value in life, panic over the effects of akathisia, and without full mental acuity, view suicide as the best or only option of deliverance. These destructive thoughts are intensified in individuals when authority figures force a person to continue consumption.

In order to better understand why suicide is increased during akathisia, one might consider the profound struggle that people trapped at high levels of the World Trade Center experienced during the September 11th attack. As these individuals found themselves being tormented by extreme levels of heat and fire, they were forced into a decision. Either they remained in their mentally and physically painful state and hoped and prayed it would soon end, or they chose to jump out of a window to escape their agonizing condition. There are numerous videos that document the many people who jumped out of Trade Center windows that day—knowing full well that they would not live. Much like those being tortured by the extreme heat produced by the plane crashes on 9/11, akathisia causes a person to both mentally and physically suffer intensely to the point of desperation.

Those who commit suicide under the influence and control of mind-altering drugs are regularly attempt to escape the drugs' toxic effects rather than life itself. Many people who are now off prescribed psychotropic drugs attest that while they were intoxicated, they would rather have died than to live in the torturous state of being under the drugs' physical and mental influence. In far too many cases, the primary motive behind suicide cannot be accurately explained apart from the influence of prescribed psychotropic drugs.

When akathisia is experienced during drug withdrawal,[25] it is the body's natural defensive reaction to a powerful foreign substance in reverse. In essence, instead of fighting the foreign chemicals, the body during withdrawal continues its fight, not realizing that the need to fight the drug's action is being diminished or has been removed. Sadly, the person's troubling response during withdrawal is often framed as evidence of further mental disorders or as a need to resume dependence upon the prescribed drug. As former President of the Royal College of Psychiatrists Wendy Burn acknowledges, the drug's withdrawal effects can be both appalling and misinterpreted as a relapse:

> Whilst the withdrawal symptoms which arise on and after stopping antidepressants are often mild and self-limiting, there can be substantial variation in people's experience, with symptoms lasting much longer and being more

---

[25] There is a growing body of evidence which suggests that many psychotropic drugs' negative effects during withdrawal—produced by their chemical properties—can last over 12 months, and some people with irreparable damage from the drugs are never able to physically recover. See Jerome Burne, "Could Antidepressants really cause brain damage? Experts reveal the pills don't work for most people and could even cause PERMANENT harm," *Daily Mail Online* (February 6, 2017): https://www.dailymail.co. uk/health/article-4197460/Could-antidepressants-damage-brain.html.

severe for some patients. Ongoing monitoring is
also needed to distinguish the features of
antidepressant withdrawal from emerging
symptoms which may indicate a relapse of
depression.[26]

It is often during times of withdrawal that suicide becomes the most attractive option, since drugs such as benzodiazepines ("benzos") can induce

acute anxiety, panic attacks, vomiting,
insomnia, muscle twitches, headaches,
paranoia, memory loss and in the most extreme
instances seizures which can cause death.[27]

---

[26] Wendy Burns, "Wendy Burns: Medical Community must ensure that those needing support to come off antidepressants can get it," *The British Medical Journal* (September 25, 2020): https://blogs.bmj.com/bmj/2020/09/25/wendy-burn-medical-community-must-ensure-that-those-needing-support-to-come-off-anti-depressants-can-get-it/.

[27] Maya Oppenheim, "Jordan Peterson suffers year of 'absolute hell' and needs emergency treatment for drug addiction that forced him to withdrawal from public life, daughter says," *The Independent* (February 8, 2020): https://www.independent.co.uk/news/world/europe/jordan-peterson-drug-addiction-benzo-valium-xanex-russia-mikhaila-a9324871.html.

Seeking out a knowledgeable physician who is comfortable with patiently deprescribing psychiatric drugs and preferably who is likeminded in faith is vitally important for anyone who desires to be freed from the toxic chemical restraints of alleged antidepressants. But even under professional supervision, many people have expressed the "hell"[28] that they endured as their bodies and minds readjusted to life free from the adverse effects of psychotropic drugs.

Unfortunately, these drugs, though framed as medicines, do not remedy a biological condition or correct an alleged chemical imbalance. There is no target disease or biological malady that they act upon, nor do they possess the ability within their chemical mechanisms to restore health to the consumer.

Moreover, applying physical and chemical restraints do not determine such treatments to be medicinal, even if applied in a medical setting by a licensed and altruistic physician. These practices, though often framed as medical treatments, can only temporarily control behavior, deescalate an emotional moment/crisis, and cripple the mind's executive control. Strapping someone to a gurney or injecting that person with tranquilizers will certainly hinder or restrain him/her from acting upon negative thoughts for a time. But the heart's desires/

---

[28] Ibid.

motives remain the root problem that must be resolved. In actuality, these drugs' mechanistic action is to agitate the nervous system and suppress mental acuity.

The evidence accrued in research and in the clinical setting have also revealed how the chemical mechanism of psychostimulants—performance enhancing drugs regularly prescribed to children with behavioral struggles—increase both the occurrence of violence and self-harm and the probability of being diagnosed with additional psychiatric labels. Several psychiatrists at the University of Colorado discuss this common problem:

> Working in an urban safety net hospital, our clinical practice is increasingly devoted to the care of patients with stimulant (methamphetamine) use disorder. In 2018, 28% of our hospital admissions involving substances were related to methamphetamines—more than twice the percentage related to opioids. **The behavioral pharmacology of methamphetamine lends itself to aggression, agitation, and violence.** Hence, these patients are often brought to care by law enforcement for disturbances in the community. **These patients then require intensive treatment given the risk of injury to themselves, other**

patients, and health care staff. Beyond the effects of acute intoxication, neurotoxic sequelae can result in disabling delusions and hallucinations that persist even after sustained sobriety and are often resistant to pharmacotherapy. This often leads to a misdiagnosis of schizophrenia or bipolar disorder. These problematic symptoms and the lack of FDA-approved treatments for methamphetamine use disorders can lead to feelings of helplessness and clinician burnout [emphasis added].[29]

While it might not be popular to expose the destructive reality of prescribed psychiatric drugs, it is certainly loving and necessary if lives are to be saved and suicide rates diminished. This is not a judgment on anyone who chooses to consume these drugs, but it is graciously informing the consumer as to what commonly occurs within the drugs' chemical actions and better equips them to make sound decisions.

---

[29] Chelsea Wolf, Melanie Rylander, Alia Al-Tayyib, and Scott Simpson, "After COVID-19 and Beyond the Opioid Wave," *Psychiatric Times* (December 29, 2020): https://www. psychiatrictimes.com/view/covid-19-beyond-opioid-wave?utm_ source=sfmc&utm_medium=email&utm_campaign=01_05_21_ PT_RegScheNL_Recruitment&eKey=ZHJiZXJnZXluZHJAZ21haWw uY29t.

It is important to reiterate that most physicians are not attempting to hurt people who are struggling with suicidal thoughts. Instead, they most likely are following how they were taught and doing their best to save lives. Yet, as popular as the medical model is within society, it has shown itself to be a failure in understanding the phenomena of suicide:

> Although patient suicide can occur across medicine, the odds are alarmingly high in psychiatry. "There's at least a 50-50 chance that a psychiatrist is going to face the suicide of a patient," says Eric Plakun, MD, medical director/CEO at the Austen Riggs Center, Stockbridge, Massachusetts, a hospital-based facility that offers a continuum of psychiatric treatment. Quoting forensic psychiatrist Robert Simon, Plakun says, "There are two kinds of psychiatrists — those who have had a patient die by suicide, and those who will."[30]

---

[30] Deborah Brauser, "Is Patient Suicide in Psychiatry a 'Medical Error'? *Medscape Psychiatry* (October 14, 2020): https://www.medscape.com/viewarticle/939130?nlid=137853_2051&src=WNL_mdplsnews_201016_mscpedit_psyc&uac=264124BV&spon=12&impID=2623271&faf=1.

No one is responsible for another person's suicide, so psychiatrists should not be held accountable for another's choices. But the system in which suicidal attempts and completions continue to increase rather than diminish and where drugs—known to increase suicidal ideation, attempts, and completions and prescribed as medicines rather than discouraged—must be denounced. Acclaimed professor of psychiatry and former consultant for the National Institute of Mental Health in America, Peter Breggin, expresses well this concern:

> Since antidepressants are now the drugs most commonly implicated in successful suicides, it would seem far more appropriate to designate them as "suicide drugs" rather than anti-suicide drugs. Yet psychiatrists persist in giving them to depressed patients who are suicidal.[31]

In the last several years, not only has there been an increase in suicidal completions in the general population,[32] but there has also been an increase in prominent evangelical pastors' taking their own lives. In almost every case, psychotropic drugs were clearly involved, yet there was hardly any mention of their

---

[31] Peter R. Breggin, *Toxic Psychiatry* (New York: St. Martin's Press, 1991), 158.

[32] "News and Comment," ANTIDEPAWARE (November 27, 2020): http://antidepaware.co.uk/news-and-comment/.

influence and contribution to suicidal ideation within published discussions that followed. Prescribing "antidepressants" may sound like a legitimate solution to the soul's deep struggles, but their chemical mechanisms have consistently shown them to be destructive rather than the alleged healing agents that the powerful pharmaceutical companies have falsely marketed them to be.[33]

If suicide is to be understood and prevented, then all potential influences must be wisely considered. Approaches which are empirically shown to be ineffective or worse still exacerbate the problem, must be eliminated. The medical model of the soul has proved itself to be one such approach that must be discarded if suicidal ideation is to be accurately explained and significantly reduced.

---

[33] For further study on how psychiatric drugs are destructive rather than healing, please see Daniel R. Berger II, *The Chemical Imbalance Delusion* (Taylors, SC: Alethia International Publications, 2019).

CHAPTER 3

A WAY OF THINKING

If suicidal ideation ("a way of thinking") is not primarily a physical problem or a medical issue, then what is the most reasonable way to understand and approach people who are struggling? The simple answer is that suicidal ideation is a way of thinking about one's self, one's relationships, and one's circumstances that is based upon the heart's desires/motives and interpretation of a person's experiences. Suicidal thinking, then, falls into the field of *phenomenology*—the study of one's perspective of his/her own soul, life, relationships, and phenomena. As with all thoughts, thinking about death apart from truth and genuine hope leads to correspondingly destructive behavior.

Although the popular medical model was examined in the previous chapter, it bears reiterating that the currently developed and allegedly scientifically-sound psychiatric tests, which are utilized in many clinics to predict suicidality, further illustrate how suicidal ideation is a metaphysical phenomenon of the soul and not a medical condition. Controlled studies repeatedly confirm that these tests fail miserably in their predictions.

The reason that these tests fail is that only a person's testimony concerning his/her own phenomenology rather than a valid biological/medical test constitutes the screening and subsequent predictive measurement. Since deceit is a primary issue of the heart in one's suicidal ideation, then the words or testimony of the individual struggling presents an unreliable predictor. One recent study, for example, which was published in *Psychosomatics: The Journal of Consultation-Liaison Psychiatry* and won the coveted Dlin/Fischer Clinical Research Award in 2020, exposed this sobering fact:

> Our finding that most patients who die by suicide deny suicide ideation in their clinical encounter is consistent with smaller prior studies. We are concerned that use of this screener may have misdirected psychiatric intervention: most patients who died by suicide screened negative (or were not screened at all) and then did not receive psychiatric care in the ED.[34]

In addition, the World Psychiatric Association reports,

---

[34] Scott Simpson, "Suicide Risk Screening Tool in Emergency Departments 'Inadequate,'" *Psychosomatics: The Journal of Consultation-Liaison Psychiatry* (September 2020): https://www .clpsychiatry.org/aclp-news/y2020/m09/dlin-fischer/.

> Finding ways to identify those at risk is a key
> public health goal, but researchers and
> clinicians alike have been stumped in the quest
> to decrease suicide rates using primary,
> secondary, and tertiary prevention strategies.
> Our predictors simply do not work well,
> especially in identifying short-term risk.[35]

The predictability of suicide when suicidal ideation is known is not a medical condition that can be diagnosed as a valid disease or in a reliable or valid way. Helping others through suicidal thinking requires spiritual discernment and the understanding of the metaphysical reality of human nature.

Suicidal ideation is a metaphysical phenomenon that is developed out of a person's view of self (identity), from his/her relationship with others, from his/her view of and reactions to the trying phenomena of life (e.g., guilt, personal struggles, "traumas"/trials, abuse, rejection, neglect, bitterness, anxiety, hopelessness, abandonment, etc.), and in accordance with his/her desires/passions/ values. Simply stated, *suicidal ideation* is a way of thinking

---

[35] Maria A. Oquendo and Enrique Baca-Garcia, "Suicidal behavior disorder as a diagnostic entity in the DSM-5 classification system: advantages outweigh limitations," *World Psychiatry: official journal of the World Psychiatric Association (WPA)* vol. 13 (2) (2014): 128-30; doi:10.1002/wps.20116.

in response to humanity's fallen nature and the fallen condition of this world post-Genesis 3. Clearly, the secular system has failed to provide valid and effective answers to suicide, because it has rejected the Creator's wisdom and design concerning the dual nature of humanity and the purpose of life.

As briefly mentioned, the field of study which seeks to understand a person's identity, his/her view of self or one's own soul, and his/her interpretation and response to the various phenomena and experiences of life is referred to as *phenomenology*. Suicidal ideation is formed through one's identity in relation to God and others, from his or her own worldview, and from his/her corresponding interpretations and explanations of and attempts to endure distressful and difficult experiences. Thus, suicidal ideation is fundamentally born out of destructive beliefs about one's own soul/life and the poor responses to life's difficult relationships and trials.

SECULAR PHENOMENOLOGY

One of the most damaging beliefs associated with suicidal ideation is the widely accepted humanistic idea that the answers to life and genuine satisfaction come from turning inward to one's own self-actualization. However, when people attempt to turn inward in order to discover both deliverance and satisfaction from humanity's broken/

fallen condition, then emptiness/vanity and potentially a hatred of life itself result.

In fact, secular research has discovered that people who "internalize" their problems are known to be more susceptible to suicidal thinking and dismissive of counseling and help from others.[36] Logically, if people are encouraged to turn inward for answers, they are in effect also encouraged to exclude external help. Tragically, humanism is a faith that teaches people to turn to their own spiritual resources for answers to and deliverance from their problems: "Strong humanistic beliefs were associated with internalizing problems."[37] Turning people inward to find answers leads them into further mental turmoil, despair, and often suicidal thinking.

As professor of philosophy and psychiatry at the University of Texas Dr. Serife Tekin recognizes, what secularists are attempting to explain in their many constructs of mental

---

[36] Matthew Sunderland and Tim Slade, "The Relationship between internalizing psychopathology and suicidality, treatment seeking, and disability in the Australian population," *Journal of Affective Disorders* (171) (January 15, 2015): 6; doi: 10.1016/j.jad.2014.09.012.

[37] W. Van der Jagty-Jelsma, M. de Vries-Schot, P. Scheepers, Pam van Deurzen, H. Klip, and J.K. Buitelaar, "Longitudinal Study of Religiosity and Mental Health of Adolescents with Psychiatric Problems. The TRAILS Study," *The Journal of European Psychiatry* vol. 45 (September 2017): 65-71; doi: 10.1016/j.eurpsy.2017.05.031.

disorders is how one's view of him/herself (identity) could be so destructive and in opposition to the evolutionary theory:

> "The question "What is the relationship between the self and mental disorder?" is especially important for mental health professionals interested in understanding and treating patients, as most mental disorders are intimately tied to self-related concerns, such as loss of self-esteem and self-control, or diminished agency and autonomy. Philosophy, along with the cognitive and behavioral sciences, offers a wealth of conceptual and empirical resources to answer this question, as the concepts of the self and psychopathology have occupied a central place in these fields since their inception. Interestingly, and unfortunately, however, scientific psychiatry, in its approach to mental disorder as primarily a cluster of signs and symptoms has been slow in acknowledging the advances in conceptualizing

and investigating mental disorders in relation to the self."[38]

A person's negative view of him/herself is often only worsened by the medical model's stigmatizing him or her as disordered and abnormal within the psychiatric diagnostic system. Being categorized in this harmful way regularly reshapes people's phenomenologies/identities/ perspective of their own souls and leaves them feeling hopeless and helpless. Though many secularists attempt to place the weight and responsibility of "stigma" onto communities,[39] the practice of categorizing people as disordered who need help and setting them aside as abnormal is profoundly a damaging act.

---

[38] Serife Tekin, "Self and Mental Disorder: Lessons for Psychiatry from Naturalistic Philosophy," *Philosophy Compass* (Wiley Online Library) (October 27, 2020): https://doi.org/10.1111/phc3.12715.

[39] "The role of stigma as a risk factor for suicide should further motivate and spur more concerted efforts to combat public stigma and support those suffering from perceived or internalized stigma . . . . As stigma may result in severe consequences, specialist care and psychological interventions should be provided to populations submitted to stigma" (Bernardo Carpiniello and Federica Pinna, "The Reciprocal Relationship between Suicidality and Stigma," *Frontiers in Psychiatry* vol. 8 [35] [March 8, 2017]: doi:10.3389/fpsyt.2017.00035).

As previously noted, humanism and its bio-psycho-social phenomenology encourages suicide both by presenting it as a dignified escape from life[40] and by promoting self-realization, self-image/esteem, and self-actualization as the highest forms of deliverance.[41] If a person's soul is struggling in despair, it does him/her no good to be told to turn inward for answers that he/she has already realized are not found in his/her own soul. Insisting that broken vessels— which all people are—find substance and satisfaction in themselves is both futile and destructive. As Solomon rightly emphasized, such attempts are vanity (2:21-23).

Not surprisingly, secular research has correlated suicidal thinking with "chronic feelings of emptiness."[42] In

---

[40] Francis Crick, B.F. Skinner, and Thomas Greening, et. al., *Humanist Manifestos I and II* edited by Paul Kurtz (Buffalo, NY: Prometheus Books, 1973), 19.

[41] For further study on this topic, see Nicolas Andre' Ellen, *Self-Esteem, Self-Image, Self-Love: How to Trade the Trinity of Self-Worship for the Triangle of Self-Evaluation* (Houston, TX: ECTC Publishing, 2020).

[42] Shirley Yen, Jessica R. Peters, Shivani Nishar, et al., "Association of Borderline Personality Disorder Criteria with Suicide Attempts: Findings from the Collaborative Longitudinal Study of Personality Disorders Over 10 Years of Follow-up," *JAMA Psychiatry* vol. 78 (2) (November 18, 2020): 187–194; doi:10.1001/jamapsychiatry.2020.3598.

Jeremiah 2:13, the prophet describes this normal/common but impairing aspect of the human condition:

> For my people have committed two evils: they
> have forsaken me, the fountain of living waters,
> and hewed out cisterns for themselves, broken
> cisterns that can hold no water.

When broken vessels strive from their own resources to provide living water that alone can satisfy and deliver the human soul from the dark waters of life and from the despair of the natural human soul, they will always come up empty and deepen their despair.

BIBLICAL PHENOMENOLOGY

The Bible clearly emphasizes that whether it is self-harm, suicidal ideation and attempts, or choices in life that may not seem to be harmful, following one's own wisdom and forsaking God's perspective of life is destructive and leads to spiritual and physical death. Proverbs 8:32-36 advises,

> And now, O sons, listen to me: blessed are
> those who keep my ways. Hear instruction and
> be wise, and do not neglect it. Blessed is the
> one who listens to me, watching daily at my
> gates, waiting beside my doors. For whoever

finds me finds life and obtains favor from the

LORD, but he who fails to find me injures

himself; all who hate me love death.

Though this passage is not specifically stating that suicide results from accepting one's own wisdom over God's, the text does make it clear that pursuing Christ and trusting in His wisdom provides spiritual life and establishes the value of temporal life. Matthew 11:29 speaks to this truth, sharing the words of Christ:

Take my yoke upon you, and learn of me; for I

am meek and lowly in heart: and ye shall find

rest unto your souls, for my yoke is easy, and

my burden is light.

In contrast to knowing and accepting the phenomenology of Christ, trusting in one's own way and rejecting God's wisdom leads to spiritual death and a hatred of life.

King Solomon provides a biblical case study of one who discovered that turning inward in his effort to find answers to life's difficulties and moral failures, and to find genuine satisfaction led him to deep despair and hatred of life rather than deliverance and fulfillment. In Ecclesiastes 1:12-15, Solomon describes the crooked nature of every person as unable to deliver him/herself from this normal but fallen condition:

I applied my heart to seek and to search out by
wisdom all that is done under heaven. It is an
unhappy business that God has given to the
children of man to be busy with. I have seen
everything that is done under the sun, and
behold, all is vanity and a striving after wind.
What is crooked cannot be made straight, and
what is lacking cannot be counted [emphasis
added].

In the remainder of chapter 1 through the end of chapter
2, Solomon recounts his precise ideations and exact efforts
to find satisfaction and deliverance—to straighten what is
crooked. Solomon's record provides an in-depth look into
how suicidal ideation is a destructive mental process and
how the thoughts lead to a person's hating life and
perceiving life to be of little or no value.

In Ecclesiastes 2:16-19, King Solomon specifically states
three things that he turned to in his own spiritual
heart/mind in attempt to escape his hopeless and
profoundly sorrowful condition: wisdom (knowledge apart
from God; facts, philosophies, and theories about the
natural world), madness/mania (the deceptive pursuit of
the heart's desires; pleasures of life), and foolishness
(one's own natural opinions and deceived perspectives)
(16-19):

I said in my heart, "I have acquired great wisdom, surpassing all who were over Jerusalem before me, and my heart has had great experience of wisdom and knowledge." **And I applied my heart to know [1] wisdom and to know [2] madness and [3] folly. I** perceived that this also is but a striving after wind. **For in much wisdom is much vexation, and he who increases knowledge increases sorrow** [emphasis added].

In chapter 2, Solomon explains how after he explored the pursuit of knowledge, he then turned to madness or what is often called "mania" within psychiatric phenomenology. Significantly, Solomon offers the exact criteria that secularists list today as constituting mania in their concepts of Bipolar I and II.[43] But as Solomon makes clear in Genesis 3, these mindsets or ideations—though destructive—are normal ways of thinking for all of humanity after the fall.

The secular psychiatric construct of "mania" further highlights how destructive self-esteem, self-actualization,

---

[43] For further study on how the constructs of bipolar I and II are secular explanations for the normal but deceived attempts of human nature to escape the sorrows of life, see Daniel R. Berger II, *Rethinking Depression: Not a Sickness, Not a Sin* (Taylors, SC: Alethia International Publications, 2019), 83-127.

and attempts at self-deliverance truly are. Secular research has consistently found that people with high self-esteem[44] are more likely to attempt suicide and are responsible for a large portion of all suicidal attempts.

> The lifetime risk of suicide in individuals with bipolar disorder is estimated to be at least 15 times that of the general population. In fact, bipolar disorder may account for one-quarter of all completed suicides.[45]

Turning people inward toward self-reliance, self-esteem, and self-actualization may sound like a good phenomenology to apply in counseling people who are struggling in despair with their own identity or who hate life, but humanism (and its bio-psycho-social phenomenology) is not medicine for the soul.

Solomon also makes it clear (2:18-26) that the end results of turning inward for answers are both a realization of life's vanity apart from God and a hatred of life itself:

---

[44] "Inflated self-esteem is typically present, ranging from uncritical self-confidence to marked grandiosity, and may reach delusional proportions" (American Psychiatric Association, *Diagnostic and Statistical Manual of Mental Disorders*, 5th ed. [Washington, DC: American Psychiatric Publishing, 2013], 128).

[45] Ibid., 131.

So I hated life, because what is done under the sun was grievous to me, for all is vanity and a striving after wind. **I hated all my toil** in which I toil under the sun, seeing that I must leave it to the man who will come after me, and who knows whether he will be wise or a fool? Yet he will be master of all for which I toiled and used my wisdom under the sun. This also is vanity. **So I turned about and gave my heart up to despair over all the toil of my labors under the sun** . . . . What has a man from all the toil and striving of heart with which he toils beneath the sun? **For all his days are full of sorrow, and his work is a vexation. Even in the night his heart does not rest.** This also is vanity.

Solomon offers deep wisdom in this context. He first explains how self-realization and self-dependence are destructive, not restorative, to the human soul. Furthermore, he exposes that having high self-esteem, even if the esteem is an accurate assessment of one's relation to others, does not deliver a person from his/her desperate state (Ecclesiastes 2:9). Moreover, Solomon correlates despair (20), self-striving after one's own desires (10-11; 21-22), and the mind's continued unrest (anxiety) as regularly causing insomnia (23). In other words, a person is negatively impaired—including in the body—by toiling to satisfy self and the deceitful desires of the flesh and by attempting to deliver one's own soul from the many problems of life.

Thankfully, Solomon's testimony of despair, which is recorded in Ecclesiastes 1-2, does not end in suicide. Rather, Solomon arrived at the realization that he must think differently than is normal about himself and life in general if he were to find value, purpose, and genuine satisfaction in his temporal life. Setting himself as his own greatest hope and claiming the pursuit of his own desires as his premiere purpose in life were Solomon's most destructive and impairing ideations. They were, in his own words, "madness"—a delusional way to approach life.

But Solomon continues in Ecclesiastes 9:3 to make the point clear that this "madness," which his own life illustrates, is the normal but "evil" reality of all humanity:

> This is an evil in all that is done under the sun,
>
> that the same event happens to all. Also, the
>
> hearts of the children of man are full of evil, and
>
> madness is in their hearts while they live, and
>
> after that they go to the dead.

Solomon not only presents madness as an unfortunate aspect of normal human nature, but he also presents death to be that as well. When people turn inward to their own souls/psyches/minds for answers, they have only madness and hopelessness to discover and the reality of death to face.

What brings about spiritual life, then, is to find the Savior who offers a supernatural phenomenology/identity/ wisdom, who provides a way through the many vexations of life, who provides truth to counter the deceitful nature of humanity's spiritual heart (Jeremiah 17:9), and who provides a purpose and meaning to life itself apart from the deceitful desires of the flesh. This Savior cannot be established upon selfish ambition or pride, but upon truth. Surely, all people need to find the unique Savior who is genuinely the only way, the only truth, and the only life.

CHAPTER 4

DEVELOPED IN THE HEART THROUGH RELATIONSHIPS

Whereas a person's turning inward to discover answers to the human problems of despair and the unfulfilled need to belong and establish meaning in life are destructive, turning to others to establish identity and meaning will either be helpful or be detrimental. This result is always dependent upon the moral quality of past and present meaningful relationships and the character of those involved. Suicidal ideation is almost always connected to one or more poor or broken relationships in the individual's life, and issues of guilt, anger/bitterness, emotional pain, rejection, legalism, and the fear of man are common struggles regularly associated with suicidal thinking. Conversely, working toward right relationships with God and fellow mankind has proved to be healing to the soul.

NEGATIVE RELATIONSHIPS

The reality that negative relationships are interconnected with suicidal ideation can be observed over 200 years ago in the words of Benjamin Rush himself. It is helpful at this point to recall that Rush was the father of John Rush, who, as historians record, attempted suicide multiple times after the traumatic duel in which John killed his best friend. There is also undeniable evidence that John struggled with feeling as though he never measured up to his father's larger than life image and expectations for him. John saw himself as "the degenerate son . . . a blackguard,"[46] which certainly influenced his consideration of suicide.[47] Though his father's attempted explanation of John's struggle was narrowly confined to speculative biological causes, the combination of John's poor/broken relationships, traumatic experience, relentless guilt, and struggles with his faith was assuredly the root cause.

Most historians today consider Dr. Rush to be one of the most important founding fathers of the medical/biological model of mental illness. While Rush's suggested medical model has failed to explain or remedy what is today framed as mental disorders, some of his observations about suicidal attempts and completions have been verified by applying the scientific method. But, as already indicated and prior to Rush's assertion of these truths, the Bible first pronounced these aspects of suicidal ideation as normal and destructive features of human nature.

---

[46] J. Jefferson Looney and Ruth L. Woodward, *Princetonians, 1791-1794* (Princeton, NJ: Princeton University Press, 1991), 435.

[47] Berger, *Saving Abnormal*, 38-40.

One of Rush's observations was that "suicidal thinking might be contagious," since he and others observed that suicidal ideation is "often propagated by means of newspapers."[48] Rush's assertion highlights how the influence of intimate relationships are central features in understanding many of the thoughts associated with suicide. What becomes evident in examining this clear correlation is that a person's consideration of suicide as a legitimate option is regularly indoctrinated by his/her hearing of or closely experiencing another's suicidal attempt or completion.

Though Rush is one of the earliest in modern day to highlight the common aspect of indoctrination involved in many suicidal attempts, the Bible first presented the reality that the influence of human associations/ relationships (as with many ways of thinking and behaving) is central to suicidal thinking. The Bible offers a clear case study in which the suicide by one is followed by the suicide of another. In 1 Samuel 31:3-5, the second suicide was clearly influenced by the first:

> The battle pressed hard against Saul, and the
> archers found him, and he was badly wounded
> by the archers. Then Saul said to his armor-

---

[48] Benjamin Rush, *An Inquiry into the Influence of Physical Causes on the Moral Faculty* (February 1786), 22.

bearer, 'Draw your sword, and thrust me
through with it, lest these uncircumcised come
and thrust me through, and mistreat me.' But
his armor-bearer would not, **for he feared
greatly**. Therefore Saul took his own sword and
fell upon it. **And when his armor-bearer saw
that Saul was dead, he also fell upon his sword
and died with him** [emphasis added].

According to the text, Saul's decision to take his own life
was based upon his fears/anxiety because of his broken
relationship to those pursuing him. The same is true for
Saul's armor-bearer, whose own suicide was likewise
based upon his fears and his relationship to Saul and the
enemy fast approaching. In both cases of suicidal attempts
and completions, fear—directly born out of a poor
relationship—was the motivating factor behind the
ideation.

By the late 1900s, it was well recognized within secular
thinking that suicidal ideation is typically influenced by a
friend, family member, or an acquaintance's similar
ideation.[49] When a clear relational connection is present
between subsequent suicides, these instances are often
referred to as "contagion" or "copycat suicides," terms

---

[49] J. Leo, "Could Suicide Be Contagious?" *Time Magazine*
(February 1986): 59.

that reflect how intimate relationships, public discourse, and indoctrination can and do shape people's thinking and corresponding behavior.[50]

In 2018, *Medscape Psychiatry* published an article which discussed how celebrity suicides increase the likelihood of copycat suicides—even influencing the means and methods of suicidal attempts:

> Not only does the suicide rate in the general population increase following a celebrity suicide, but victims copy the method, new research shows. Investigators found that in the weeks following the death of actor and comedian Robin Williams on August 11, 2014, which was widely reported as a suicide by hanging, there was a surge in suicides by hanging.[51]

It is not merely the ideas that are transmitted; it is also the precise methods. Through close or valued relationships, a shared phenomenology is most often established. When that phenomenology is rooted in deceitful thinking, it

---

[50] Ibid.

[51] Pauline Anderson, "Celebrity Suicides Trigger Copycat Deaths by Same Method," *Medscape Psychiatry* (May 10, 2018): https://www.medscape.com/viewarticle/896452#vp_2.

often produces patterns of destructive behavior in spheres of influence and even in large populations. Many middle and high schools see groups of students simultaneously struggling with suicidal thoughts—especially if there has been a recent attempt or completion within the student body. Many times, school administrators feel as though suicide awareness is needed to help deal with the growing issue. But in reality, these times of indoctrination often worsen the problem.

The fact that exposure to suicide without discerning conversations is regularly damaging must be further examined. In 2017, a *Netflix* series entitled *13 Reasons Why* discussed in detail how various poor relationships can lead many people to consider suicide. The drama—said to teach suicide awareness—was widely viewed, especially by teenagers and young adults, and the following months confirmed once again that the indoctrination of suicidal thinking is common:

> In the month following the show's debut in March 2017, there was a 28.9% increase in suicide among Americans ages 10-17, said the study, published in the *Journal of the American academy of Child and Adolescent Psychiatry*. The number of suicides was greater than that seen in any single month over the five-year period researchers examined. Over the rest of

the year, there were 195 more youth suicides than expected given historical trends.[52]

As critics noted, *13 Reasons Why* offered no reasons why someone should not commit suicide; the show only provided both a descriptive psychology/phenomenology whereby people could identify and a lens from which to evaluate their own relationships in a similar way. When the viewers identified with the actors, their suicidal ideation also increased. What the empirical data from research reveals is that the more "aware" a person becomes of suicide apart from truth that can set one free from deceitful thinking, apart from meaningful relationships that are restorative, and apart from genuine hope for life's deep struggles, the more detrimental it is to the one who listens and is willing to consider this act as potentially beneficial for him/herself.

Adding to the false belief that suicide represents a legitimate escape from life is the common but false image of victimhood in which the deceased are spoken of as a "victim of suicide." When humanistic teaching is accepted, people are more likely to view suicide as a dignified escape or as something that could not be helped. While it is

---

[52] Matthew S. Swartz, "Teen Suicide Spiked After Debut of Netflix's '13 Reasons Why,' Study Says," *NPR Mental Health* (April 30, 2019): https://www.npr.org/2019/04/30/718529255/teen-suicide-spiked-after-debut-of-netflixs-13-reasons-why-report-says.

certainly right to eulogize and honor the deceased for the life that they lived, dignifying suicide is morally wrong and leads others who are already struggling to consider suicide as a legitimate escape from their own problems. Such an approach treats suicide as if it were the "Grim Reaper" who stole a life against the person's will. Unfortunately, this wrong perspective dominates psychiatric theory.[53] Campaigns that center on "suicide awareness" regularly promote the destructive ideation (likely unintentionally) rather than discourage people from it, and many universities that organize campus days and events that are dedicated to suicidal awareness see a significant increase in suicidal ideation, attempts, and completions on those scheduled days and in the weeks shortly after.

Many times, relationships and indoctrination are entirely overlooked as contributing to suicidal ideation, and sometimes they are outright denied. The National Alliance on Mental Illness (NAMI), for example, asserts on its website that

> there is a widespread stigma associated with
> suicide and as a result, many people are afraid
> to speak about it. Talking about suicide not only
> reduces the stigma, but also allows individuals

---

[53] Kristen Fuller, "5 Common Myths about Suicide Debunked," *NAMI* (September 30, 2020): https://www.nami.org/Blogs/NAMI-Blog/September-2020/5-Common-Myths-About-Suicide-Debunked.

to seek help, rethink their opinions and share
their story with others. We all need to talk more
about suicide.[54]

Discussing suicide apart from life-giving truth, though, is naturally destructive.

In 2019, a popular American pastor, Jarrid Wilson, tragically took his own life, which prompted much media attention and talk within Christian circles. This particular suicide was one of many in Christendom over a three-year span, which included several well-known pastors. Sadly, many people within the Christian community presented these pastors as "victims of suicide." As tragic as each case was, each suicide was an individual choice. A person not intimately connected with these pastors can only wonder how these seemingly separate cases influenced the others and whether they could continue to influence more people if not graciously and biblically addressed.

We do know specifics about this phenomenon, however, that illuminate Jarrid Wilson's (and others) suicidal ideation, attempt, and death. Wilson's suicide occurred in less than 24 hours of his presiding over the funeral of a lady in his church who had committed suicide. Furthermore, he had posted over 15 social media posts in the two weeks leading to his death that promoted "suicide

---

[54] Ibid.

awareness." He was also taking "antidepressants"—widely known to increase suicidal ideation. The combination of struggling with the sorrow of pastoring and constantly dealing with broken relationships, facing a close family member or friend's own death, dealing with the negative influence of psychotropic drugs, battling the sinful struggles and subsequent guilt that all Christians face, and dwelling on suicide apart from God's grace can culminate in shaping a person's view of him/herself and the phenomena of life. Significant relationships can and regularly do negatively impact one's phenomenology/ worldview.

Because of the clear correlation between suicidal thinking and close relationships, many materialists insist—apart from any empirical evidence—that the connections which occur within the same family provide evidence that justifies their theory that suicidal ideation and suicidal completions are a genetically inherited disorder. For this reason, suicidal thoughts are often stated as "suicidal tendencies." For example, one book entitled *The Neurobiological Basis of Suicide* offers this common secular perspective:

> Suicide is complex, multifactorial behavioral phenotype. Suicide is also familial: **a family history of suicide increases risk of suicide attempts and completed suicide.** In this chapter, we will examine the family, twin, and

74

adoption studies that establish the existence of both genetic and environmental bases of suicidal behavior.[55]

Though these authors do admit that suicidal ideation is first and foremost a complex metaphysical phenomenon that often results in outworking behavior ("a behavioral phenotype"), they insist—in accordance with their reductionistic faith—that suicide be viewed as a biological/genetic problem. But if behavior and ways of thinking are learned through watching a fictional TV series or learning of the suicide of one's favorite celebrity, then those mindsets are even more influenced by the intimate relationship and loss of a dear loved one.

Materialists are often guilty of passing over the simplest explanation in attempt to uphold their faith. Just as they ignore that behavior is primarily learned, they also see patterns of similar occupations within generations as hereditarily caused rather than relationally learned. For instance, an article published in the *British Medical Journal* asserted that because many families continue through

---

[55] Clement C Zai, Vincenzo de Luca, John Strauss, Ryan P. Tong, Isaac Sakinofsky, and James L. Kennedy, "Genetic Factors and Suicidal Behavior," *The Neurobiological Basis of Suicide* edited by Dwivedi Y, editor (Boca Raton, FL: CRC Press/Taylor & Francis, 2012), chapter 11; https://www.ncbi.nlm.nih.gov/books/NBK107191/.

generations to become physicians, becoming a medical doctor must be genetic.[56]

Relationships that involve indoctrination, not genetics, best explain copycat and familial suicides. Just as a child learns to speak the same primary language of his/her primary caregiver or to value and cheer on the same sport's team as his/her parents or friends, ideations and behaviors are most readily learned through significant and close relationships.

To further illustrate this reality, suicidal ideation and completions can also be observed in large groups of people. Though many cults throughout history offer prime examples, one of the most well-known mass suicides occurred at the infamous Jonestown episode:[57]

> Although Jones's followers would later be
> stereotyped as sinister, brainwashed idiots, the

---

[56] Maria Polyakova, Petra Persson, Katja Hofmann, and Anupam B. Jena, and Ruth L Newhouse, "Does Medicine Run in the Family—evidence from three generations of physicians in Sweden: retrospective observational study," *BJM* 371 (December 16, 2020): https://doi.org/10.1136/bmj.m4453.

[57] J Oliver Conroy, "An apocalyptic cult, 900 dead: remembering the Jonestown massacre, 40 years on," *The Guardian* (November 17, 2018): https://www.theguardian.com/world/2018/nov/17/an-apocalyptic-cult-900-dead-remembering-the-jonestown-massacre-40-years-on.

journalist Tim Reiterman argues in his seminal book on the subject that many were "decent, hardworking, socially conscious people, some highly educated", who "wanted to help their fellow man and serve God, not embrace a self-proclaimed deity on earth". The Peoples Temple advocated socialism and communitarian living and was racially integrated to an exceptional standard rarely matched since . . . Back at Jonestown, Jones announced that it was time to undertake the final "white night". To quell disagreement, he told inhabitants that Congressman Ryan had already been murdered, sealing the commune's fate and making "revolutionary suicide" the only possible outcome. The people of Jonestown, some acceptant and serene, others probably coerced, queued to receive cups of cyanide punch and syringes.[58]

Mass suicides reflect how relationships help to shape people's ways of thinking and their corresponding behaviors—even those choices which are rooted in deceit and are destructive and unseemly.

---

[58] Ibid.

Another recollection of a famous mass suicide that offers insight into this aspect of normal human nature, but which occurred apart from any cultish teaching, is the Jewish historian Josephus Flavius' account of Masada:

> With Jerusalem in ruins, the Romans turned their attention to taking down Masada, the last community in Judea with 960 rebels, including many women and children. Led by Flavius Silva, a legion of 8,000 Romans built camps surrounding the base, a siege wall, and a ramp on a slope of the Western side of the mountain made of earth and wooden supports. After several months of siege without success, the Romans built a tower on the ramp to try and take out the fortress's wall. When it became clear that the Romans were going to take over Masada, on April 15, 73 A.D., on the instructions of Ben Yair, all but two women and five children, who hid in the cisterns and later

told their stories, took their own lives rather than live as Roman slaves.[59]

Both the established relationships of the people and their shared fear/anxiety led to a disturbing conclusion of their lives.

Additionally, "a person's relationship difficulties" also increases the likelihood of suicidal ideation and attempts.[60] Many who contemplate suicide feel alone or rejected, fear the rejection or disapproval of others, have been deeply hurt by others, or have through their own choices and actions cut off significant relationships in their lives. The fear of man, which the Bible makes clear is like a mental trap or prison that isolates and destroys the soul (Proverbs 29:25), is a common struggle. Because wise counselors should consider that those who contemplate suicide have relational problems that need to be resolved, they must evaluate and address any toxic or broken

---

[59] Flavius Josephus quoted by the editors, "Masada," *History* (March 4, 2019): https://www.history.com/topics/ancient-middle-east/masada.

[60] Batya Swift Yasgur, "Three Factors Tied to Higher Suicide Risk in Borderline Personality Disorder," *Medscape Psychiatry* (November 27, 2020): https://www.medscape.com/viewarticle/941686?nlid= 138509_424&src=WNL_mdplsfeat_201201_ms cpedit_psyc&uac=264124BV&spon=12&impID=2710242&faf=1# vp_2.

relationships that have fostered destructive and deceitful thinking.

POSITIVE RELATIONSHIPS

While negative relationships have proved to be destructive and regularly promote suicidal ideation, relationships that are focused on establishing meaningful connections, expressing empathy, and offering hope have been shown to provide help to those who are suicidal. *JAMA Psychiatry* published an article in late 2020, which again affirmed the important correlation between a person's relationships and his/her struggle with suicidal thoughts:

> Adults who perceived a higher level of social support reported fewer depressive and anxiety symptoms 1 year later, after adjustment for sex and all remaining confounders, including previous MHPs . . . . Individuals who perceived more social support were also less likely to report suicidal ideation (vs those with no suicidal ideation) and less likely to attempt suicide (vs no attempts), and these associations remained even after adjusting for the potential

confounders, including previous MHPs and suicidal ideation and attempts.[61]

When people find comfort, support, and meaning within their communities, they are less likely to consider suicide.

When suicidal thinking is present, it is highly likely that broken relationships will need to be acknowledged and by God's grace restored. A person's identity cannot be separated from his/her relationships both with God and with others, and counselors who wish to truly deal with the heart of suicide should make great effort to explore these vital aspects of being human.

Counselors are also wise to establish a meaningful relationship built upon trust and biblical love with those that they counsel. More than anything that could be initially said, showing another person genuine care and concern has been shown to be helpful for those ruminating over taking their own lives.

In a recent study, people struggling with suicidal ideation reported a significant diminished desire to take their own lives after calling a suicide hotline and talking with a

---

[61] Sara Scardera, Lea C. Perret, Isabelle Ouellet-Morin, et al., "Association of Social Support During Adolescence with Depression, Anxiety, and Suicidal Ideation in Young Adults," *JAMA Psychiatry* (December 4, 2020): doi:10.1001/jama networkopen.2020.27491.

person who in their estimation seemed to care, and they reported even less of a suicidal inclination when they received a call back days later from the same individual. Those who had been considering suicide gave testimony that they felt valued and loved when they perceived that someone cared.[62] Truly, relational struggles, rejection, abuse, and abandonment are key influences in suicidal attempts.

Because God designed humanity to flourish in right moral relationships, people need assurance of not only their own significance as a loved child of God but also the meaning of life that is derived from right relationships. It is no surprise, then, to learn that even secular research has confirmed this reality:

> The researchers found it was critical for counselors to quickly establish a rapport with callers by treating them with respect and empathy. "If they didn't do that in the first 3 minutes, they were less likely to have a positive effect," Mishara says. The most effective counselors then worked with callers to explore

---

[62] Greg Miller, "Three Suicide Prevention Strategies Show Real Promise. How Can They Reach More People?" *Science Magazine* (August 22, 2019): https://www.sciencemag.org/news/2019/08/three-suicide-prevention-strategies-show-real-promise-how-can-they-reach-more-people.

alternatives to suicide, asking how they'd dealt
with past crises or who in their lives could
help.[63]

By being empathetic and sympathetic, while charting a
positive way through the darkness (establishing some form
of hope), complete strangers can impact a person's life in
an affirmative way and provide comfort and significant
connections.[64]

Numerous military projects, which were created as
attempts to reduce veteran suicide rates, have also
concluded that supportive relationships better enable
people to deal with their poor thinking in a practical and
orderly manner and to realize that suicide is not a
legitimate option to consider. Military journalist Hope
Hodge Seck offers insight into one such program, *The
Warrior Care Network*:

The members get to know each other deeply
and participate in one another's healing. And

---

[63] Greg Miller, "Three Suicide Prevention Strategies Show
Real Promise. How Can They Reach More People?" *Science
Magazine* (August 22, 2019): https://www.sciencemag.org/
news/2019/08/three-suicide-prevention-strategies-show-real-
promise-how-can-they-reach-more-people.

[64] While it important to offer hope, false hopes can end up
causing worse despair and are in the end destructive (Proverbs
13:12).

they may play a role in the program's 92% graduation rate—well above the 30-50% completion rate for conventional therapy, Home Base staff said. Even though participants are often pushed to the point of quitting, they'll work through the pain and discomfort rather than give up on their teammates, staff say. "They stay to help each other," said Dr. Thomas Spencer, chief medical director. " . . . **We can all see something in each other that we can't see in ourselves."** They graduate together in an emotional ceremony, and stay connected via a specially created closed Facebook group as they return to jobs, responsibilities and the pace of everyday life [emphasis added].[65]

Other studies conducted within various military branches have also shown the effectiveness of having someone care enough to participate in the experience of the counselee through empathic listening:

---

[65] Hope Hodge Seck, "This Squad PTSD Therapy Runs Just 2 Weeks. And It's Changing Vet's Lives," *Military* (November 14, 2019): https://www.military.com/daily-news/2019/11/14/squad-style-ptsd-therapy-runs-just-2-weeks-and-its-changing-vets-lives.html.

Social support provides a valuable element in suicide intervention and prevention. In fact, psychotherapeutic experience provides the most powerful evidence for the main purpose of social support – that of listening. **It is active listening and consequent proactive contributions by an educated social support team that provides the compassionate understanding needed to combat persistent hopelessness and helplessness** . . . . The military and the civilian community have missed the mark on suicide intervention and prevention. The truly intervening and healing elements are not treatment programs, not piles of pills, not being encouraged time and again to reach out...**but community itself, in the context of compassionate, educated, reciprocal, PROACTIVE social support** [emphasis added].[66]

Relationships, as God designed them, are intended to point those in the relationships to the God of true love and

---

[66] Randi J. Jensen and Katherine T. Platoni, "Most Military Efforts Miss Target on Suicide Preventions," *The National Psychologist* (November 21, 2018): https://nationalpsychologist. com/2018/11/most-military-efforts-miss-target-on-suicide-prevention/105185.html.

the giver and architect of life itself. Relationships, for better or for worse, are major influences in the formation of our phenomenologies/identities.

It is certainly beneficial for human relationships to be established in genuine empathy, but actually finding value, joy, positive identity, deliverance, and satisfaction in life comes from intimately connecting with God and His people, since it is God who is the living water with which broken vessels desperately desire to be filled. If relationships are not established according to God's design and wisdom, then dark waters will inevitably fill one's soul.

This reality about human nature is illustrated in the life of the Apostle Paul, who emphasized that he himself had been comforted by God and was then able to offer the same comfort to others who were likewise battling deep despair and facing death (2 Corinthians 1:3-9). Without considering God, who is love and truth and in whose image we are made, comforting others and being compassionate toward them offers no hope of an enduring solution. This determines that the church—God's people—be instrumental in helping souls to fear God rather than other mortals. Churches and homes where legalism, authoritarianism, corruption, abuse, bitterness, etc. are commonplace—instead of being a place of encouragement and edification—can and regularly do foster suicidal thinking. If the church is to help diminish or resolve suicidal ideations, they must be transparent about their brokenness and humbly promote the fear of the Lord and

His wisdom that brings about the richness of life and relationships as God intends (Proverbs 1:1-7; 22:4).

But it must be made clear that each person is responsible for his/her own decisions. While churches, families, friends, authority figures/idols, humanistic schools, psychiatric labels, and even national media organizations can and regularly do influence people's wrong ways of thinking about themselves and their lives, each person ultimately determines his/her phenomenology and determines his/her own choices. Influences are important to consider, but the motives of the heart are in the end the cause.

Still, for better or for worse, relationships are central to the human condition, to one's identity/phenomenology, and to life itself. All relationships contain some expression of discipleship. God designed individuals to thrive in righteous relationships with Him and with other people, and each relationship either points us toward the One who is life and the giver of it or toward the way that naturally seems right to people but ends in death (Proverbs 14:12).

CHAPTER 5

FOUNDED IN DECEITFUL THINKING

Many believe that when individuals complete a suicide attempt, those tragic deaths were the result of hopelessness or the product of depression. Certainly, the struggle with hopelessness is a key issue in suicidal thinking. But most often the consideration to commit suicide also involves a deceitful way of thinking rather than just an obvious state of despair.

One of the most common ways people are deceived into considering suicide is the false hope of self-deliverance. Essentially, to take one's own life is to place dependence upon oneself, and such a destructive belief is rooted in the natural deceit of the spiritual heart.

When someone considers suicide apart from the toxic control of psychotropic drugs, it is a clear indication that a person's core struggle rests within his/her identity and in a false trusting in his/her own abilities, efforts, resources, and beliefs to find a fulfilling life and to be delivered from humanity's universal fallen condition. This fact illuminates why anxiety is regularly associated with suicidal ideation. Anxiety is a person's natural and honest realization that life is not going his/her way or might not, that he/she is not in control of desired outcomes, and thus that he/she is not the sovereign God over life as all people desire to be. When people acknowledge their limitations to secure desired outcomes or fear losing what they value, they struggle with anxiety. This mental state, though distressing, is both normal and an honest reflection of the human condition.

The correlations between anxiety stemming from self-focus and suicidal ideation also explains why the suicide rate is so high among people diagnosed within psychiatric phenomenology as having bipolar (I or II), borderline personality, or other similarly alleged disorders where self-focus and self-image is a central characteristic.[67] When a person is struggling with "too high self-esteem,"[68] as the *DSM-5* acknowledges in many of its published diagnostic constructs, he or she is more likely to also struggle with suicidal ideation. Thinking highly of one's self, passionately pursuing selfish ambitions, and believing one's self to have the resources within one's own intellect and efforts for realization of and deliverance from life's fallen condition constitute a delusional and destructive approach to life. Suicide is regularly the horrific final step in the delusional

---

[67] Shirley Yen, Jessica R. Peters, Shivani Nishar, et al., "Association of Borderline Personality Disorder Criteria with Suicide Attempts: Findings From the Collaborative Longitudinal Study of Personality Disorders Over 10 Years of Follow-up," *JAMA Psychiatry* vol. 78 (2) (November 18, 2020): 187–194; doi:10.1001/jamapsychiatry.2020.3598.

[68] APA, *DSM-5*, 128.

belief that one can rescue him/herself from despair and can somehow produce a satisfying life free from trials.

But despair itself needs further examination. Editor in Chief Emeritus of the *Psychiatric Times* Ronald Pies conveys his own thoughts on this destructive state of mind:

> Despair is understood broadly as "an entire
> want of hope." I believe Gilbert is correct in
> conceptualizing this as an existential problem—
> with important implications for psychiatry.[69]

Pies notes further in the article that current research indicates that both substance use and suicide rates are commonly linked to despair. In one particular study published in *JAMA*, researchers offered "7 indicators of despair:" feelings of hopelessness, helplessness, feeling unloved or worthless, experiencing worry, self-pity, and loneliness.[70] Despair is the natural but deceitful and destructive human tendency to look inward for

---

[69] Ronald Pies, "Psychiatry and the Dark Night of the Soul," *Psychiatric Times* (December 14, 2020): https://www.psychiatric times.com/view/psychiatry-dark-night-soul.

[70] Copeland, W. E., Gaydosh, L., Hill, S. N., Godwin, J., Harris, K. M., Costello, E. J., & Shanahan, L., "Associations of Despair With Suicidality and Substance Misuse Among Young Adults," *JAMA* vol. *3* (6) (June 2020): e208627. https://doi.org/10.1001/jamanetworkopen.2020.8627.

strength/help, worth, comfort, satisfaction, and a positive future, when life is distressful, sorrowful, traumatic, or not unfolding as desired. Despair is a normal mental state of hopelessness and helplessness, as a person arrives at perceiving no future for him/herself and believing that no one can help; it is a state of the human soul that cries out for deliverance and desperately searches for a Savior.

In many cases, despair is revealed in how people deceitfully convince themselves that no one wants them around, that they are worthless, or that they are a burden to others.

> From the sufferers' perspective, their self-worth may be so low, their outlook so bleak, that their families/friends/fans would be a lot better off without them in the world, ergo their suicide is actually intended as an act of generosity?[71]

There are many deceitful ways of thinking that can lead people to engage in destructive behavior. Many secularists insist that the deceitfulness of the heart sometimes represents an abnormality ("a disorder") in those who consider suicide. But as Scripture asserts, all people are

---

[71] Dean Burnett, "Robin William's Death: A Reminder that Suicide and Depression are not Selfish," *The Guardian* (August 2014): https://www.theguardian.com/science/brain-flapping /2014/aug/12/robin-williams-suicide-and-depression-are-not-selfish.

naturally deceived in various destructive ways (e.g., Jeremiah 17:9; Ecclesiastes 9:3).

As previously mentioned, the Apostle Paul's personal struggle with despair, recorded in 2 Corinthians 1:8-10, offers the only viable solution and an alternative to turning to oneself or other false hopes when wrestling in profound times of hopelessness and helplessness:

> For we do not want you to be unaware, brothers, of the affliction we experienced in Asia. **For we were so utterly burdened beyond our strength that we despaired of life itself. Indeed, we felt that we had received the sentence of death. But that was to make us rely not on ourselves but on God who raises the dead.** He delivered us from such a deadly peril, and he will deliver us. On him we have set our hope that he will deliver us again [emphasis added].

When people despair of life (for various reasons), they must establish hope if they are to move forward and attempt to discover deliverance. As president of the American Psychiatric Association Dilip Jeste acknowledges, hope must be established within a person's beliefs if suicidal thoughts are to be diminished or eliminated.[72]

But false hopes can never deliver the soul from despair, guilt, and the very real turmoil of life. Instead, false hopes, though they can sustain the human soul for a short time, will always fail in the end. When a person's hopes are revealed to be false and understood to never be able to satisfy—"they are deferred," they always worsen the condition of the spiritual heart (Proverbs 13:12). Deceitful thinking, even in the establishment of false hopes, is ultimately destructive to the human soul.

If both hopelessness (despair or a crushed spirit) and false hopes (including suicidal ideation) are to be remedied, then only the establishment of genuine hope that will bring about joy and satisfaction can correct suicidal ideation. If life lacks sure value, clear purpose as designed, and a secure way forward—"an anchor for the soul," then people cannot find a rational reason to live.

Thankfully, Scripture presents the only genuine hope known to mankind, as biblical figures such as Job and Paul attested to in their own deep experiences of despair. Most

---

[72] "Behavioral change is our expertise. When people are suicidal, we give them hope," (Dilip V. Jeste, "On the State of Psychiatry," *Current Psychiatry 19 [12]* [December 19, 2020]: 34-36; also available from: https://www.mdedge.com/ psychiatry/ article/232726 /dilip-v-jeste-md-state-psychiatry/ page/0/2).

English Bible translations do not use the term "hopelessness," though its counterpart, "hope," is a central theme throughout Scripture. Actually, a "crushed spirit" and "despair" are the biblical phrases which English translations regularly utilize to describe the humbling and crippling mental, emotional, and behavioral effects of being honest about the very real fallen condition of humanity and the unbearable weight of the world in which everyone lives apart from the security of guaranteed deliverance and the sure future of satisfaction in Christ.

Proverbs 18:14 illustrates how hopelessness and is not primarily a biological problem but is a spiritual realization: "A man's spirit will endure sickness, but a **crushed spirit who can bear** [emphasis added]?" When people arrive at a spiritual/mental point of perceiving their only hope to be the ending of their own lives, they have reached the state of exhausting all other possible efforts and resources which they might consider to be able to rescue them from despair. Yet, as Scripture makes clear, when the full reality of hopelessness and helplessness apart from Christ is realized, no one can spiritually/mentally shoulder its weight on his/her own. God did not design people to be their own Savior or comforter, and all human attempts to deliver the soul from weakness and wickedness will always fail.

Suicide is driven by false beliefs. Some of the most common beliefs within this ideation are that "I am my best means of hope and deliverance from my own fallen condition and the fallen world in which I live," that "life should be within my own control and apart from suffering," that "I will do others a favor by taking my own life," and that "If I cannot have my desires fulfilled, then there is no way forward or reason to live." These deceitful ways of thinking (and others) require that a person do all that he/she can within his/her own resources to be one's own sovereign savior. This ideation is a destructive delusion.

CHAPTER 6

NOT THE END OF SORROW OR DESPAIR

Contrary to the false beliefs of many who end up committing suicide, the act of taking one's own life does not end the experienced despair and deep sorrow of life; it is not a valid escape. Rather, when a person commits suicide, he/she transfers his/her despair, sorrow, and mental turmoil to those who are left behind.[73] In many ways, acting as one's own Savior and attempting to deliver oneself from the evil of this world instead of bearing the sorrows of others, as the one true Savior did for his people (Isaiah 53), forces others to bear the deep sorrows of those who are departed.

Suicide is not only steeped in deceit but is also self-centered at its core, since it fails to prefer loved ones and

---

[73] "Emotions and Challenges" (2020): https://allianceofhope.org/emotions-challenges.

deeply hurts nearly everyone who is left behind.[74] It is argued by many secularists that "suicide is not selfish," since they perceive that the motives of many people who attempt suicide claim to do so in deference to others in their lives.[75] As discussed in the previous chapter, however, this motive is born in the deceitfulness of the heart. To state that suicide is selfish is not to judge a person's motives. Instead, it is to expose the inevitable result of a completed suicide. Trauma, guilt, remorse, deep pain, shame, and even one's own mental battle with the meaning of life are common struggles of survivors with a family member or friend who successfully completed a suicide attempt.

Worse still, if the one who commits suicide is not a Christian, then his/her despair and torment will only

---

[74] It is worth noting that many people who professionally enter the fields of psychiatry, counseling, clinical psychology, psychotherapy, and social work (according to their own testimonies) do so based upon having survived a traumatic event in their own lives, and many times, the motivating event was the completed suicide of a loved one or friend. Suicide is always relational. Choosing to take one's own life directly affects those around a person in negative ways and might even unintentionally establish a dreadful example for siblings and close friends to follow.

[75] Kristen Fuller, "5 Common Myths about Suicide Debunked," *NAMI* (September 30, 2020): https://www. nami.org/Blogs/NAMI-Blog/September-2020/5-Common-Myths-About-Suicide-Debunked.

intensify at the point of death. The false promise that death will end suffering and provide an escape from sorrow, guilt, and turmoil is often the thought process behind suicide attempts. But according to the Word of God, unbelievers will not escape the torment and despair of eternity in the Lake of Fire when they die.

Because Christ is the only all-sufficient sacrifice that takes away the sins of the world (John 1:29; 36), it is Christ's sacrificing his own physical life that brings about spiritual life for those who accept this payment. It is no wonder, then, that Christ does not ask the believer to die for Him, but to be a living sacrifice (Romans 12:1-4) who daily denies him/herself and who takes up his/her own cross to follow Christ (Luke 9:23).

Since living for oneself is destructive to self and others, suicide is a false gospel which insists that by a person's laying down his/her physical life for him/herself, that person can not only find the spiritual life that everyone deeply desires to experience but also can show love to others.

Suicide not only falsely takes responsibility for the atoning of sin, appeasement of guilt, the relief of suffering, and the bearing of sorrows caused by fallen experiences (Isaiah 53), but it also forgoes loving others—even if the individual claim's an unselfish motive. John 15:13 offers this insight: "Greater love has no one than this, that someone lay down his life for his friends." Many deceitfully think that taking his/her own life makes him/her into a victim or "relieves others of the burden of his/her life." In essence, though, such thinking distorts the truth about the vicarious atonement of Christ and offers those left behind deep pain and suffering rather than the deep love of Christ.

In contrast to the false gospel that is suicide, Jesus Christ is the only true victim, the only one who perfectly laid down his life as an atonement for sin, the only acceptable guilt offering, the complete comforter and bearer of sorrows, and the only genuine hope for guaranteed deliverance from suffering and condemnation.[76] Without a life lived in identity with Christ and for Him by grace through faith, life cannot make sense and lacks restorative meaning. At its core, suicide is a false gospel that promises ineffectually to make all things new.

---

[76] Genuine Christians can commit suicide, since deceitfulness, selfish ambition, and violence are in the natural hearts of everyone, even after conversion. Add to this reality the destructive, distressful, and mind-controlling effects of psychotropic drugs within a person's nervous system, and a Christian's suicidal ideations are easily understood. Roman Catholicism has traditionally taught that those who commit suicide lose their opportunity to go to Heaven. Yet, like many Roman Catholic doctrines, this way of thinking is not based upon Scripture, but upon self-established authority and philosophies of men apart from God's Inspired Word. Still, to commit suicide is not in accordance with God's will.

CHAPTER 7

NOT ALL THE SAME

The reality that people struggle with suicidal thinking for different reasons reveals that suicidal thinking is not a "one size fits all" problem. Some people will arrive at a desire to take their own life because of the seemingly insurmountable guilt of their past sins, while others will struggle without the hope of being delivered from their fears, anxieties, and distressing memories formed after surviving a traumatic experience. Some will struggle with the constant mental failure to live up to their parent's or their own perfectionistic ideals. Still others will become desperate in an intoxicated state under the horrific influence of powerful psychiatric drugs. As will be emphasized further in the next chapter, there is always a motive of the heart that leads a person to consider suicide, and it is up to those with discernment to graciously find the root struggle of the heart as they counsel those in need. Counselors must understand that there always exists a reason/purpose for which a person is contemplating and verbalizing a potential suicide, and that this motive (s) must be realized and graciously/biblically addressed.

When researchers attempt to answer the "why" question or discover the reasons people commit suicide, they first look for correlations. Though statistics and patterns are sometimes helpful in understanding motives and causes, correlates do not always indicate causality. For example, many researchers have discovered within their own work that suicide regularly occurs when a person is incarcerated for committing a crime:

> Although these numbers of deaths by suicide are shocking, they are not surprising. Past studies have found that suicide is the leading cause of death in jails and makes up more than one-third of all deaths in jails. Studies have also found that the initial pre-trial lockup period, which is the interval immediately following arrest and booking, is associated with a particularly high rate of suicide . . . . The study reveals that recent arrest status is associated with higher prevalence of suicide attempts than parole, probation, or no involvement with the criminal justice system. In this population, the highest prevalence of suicide (ie, the group with recent arrest) also had the highest prevalence of substance use disorders. Earlier studies have identified an increased risk of drug-related death following release from correctional facilities. **These**

studies reveal that the period after recent arrest may be a particularly vulnerable time for suicide. Although more research is needed, a hypothesis for this is that a recent arrest is a unique stressor that contributes to suicide risk [emphasis added].[77]

The author's assumed correlate—though she attests to her lack of confidence in her own conclusion—is the distress of being arrested. But there are many other motives to consider. Understanding that motives and mindsets differ among different people allows one to observe that guilt over the crime committed, hopelessness and anxiety over the potential loss of freedom, damage to one's moral view of his/herself, anxiety over the pending trial, and the loss of and/or damage to desired relationships are all factors to consider as to why people commit suicide upon entering the criminal justice system. If anything, the increase in suicidal thinking and behavior upon incarceration illustrates how all these ideas/motives of the spiritual heart can merge in the mind, so that people deceitfully view suicide as a reasonable act.

---

[77] Jennifer Piel, "Suicide Risk Following Criminal Arrest," *Psychiatric Times* (December 30, 2020): https://www.psychiatric times.com/view/suicide-risk-following-criminal-arrest?utm_ source=sfmc&utm_medium=email&utm_campaign=01_05_21_ PT_RegScheNL_Recruitment&eKey=ZHJiZXJnZXluZHJAZ21haWw uY29t.

Seasoned counselors are well aware that there are a few people who use the threat of suicide as a way of attracting attention. These are individuals who are sometimes regulars to the emergency room or to the pastor's office. Yet, each of them has no intention of ending his/her life. Others are not after attention as much as they are desirous to get their own way, and threatening suicide is one of their choice tools for manipulating others.

The majority of people, however, who express a desire to attempt suicide are typically not doing so because they are seeking attention. It is dangerous and irresponsible, then, to assume that a person's confession of suicidal ideation is merely to get attention or is a form of manipulation. When a person shares that he/she has been contemplating suicide, it is always best to treat it as a genuine expression of that person's spiritual heart and a choice that he/she is seriously considering. Over time, the true motive of the heart will likely be revealed.

In an effort to discover a person's spiritual heart and unique history, counselors must be careful that counseling does not resemble a criminal investigation, but rather that it is characterized by biblical discipleship or evangelism. When a person in need of help and those attempting to help him/her—whether parents or others—become at odds with each other, humility and thus transparency will surely be absent, and the broken relationship may push the one in need to further consider suicide.

Moreover, if trust and biblical love are not central to counseling, then transparency and thus the opportunity to discern the heart's motives will likely be absent. It is vital that the counselors be relational and apply considerable discernment in order to get to the heart of suicidal thinking in each individual.

CHAPTER 8

THE SCRIPTURE SPEAKS

Because the Bible discusses and offers wisdom concerning all human phenomena which occur in the soul/psyche, both deep thoughts of despair and death as well as more specific suicidal ideations and completions are found in Scripture. It is vital to examine and distinguish between the history of people who are documented in the Bible as struggling with desiring death and those the Word of God records who not only struggled with despair but also seriously considered taking or took their own lives. These passages along with others (some previously referenced) offer insight into both the thought processes in the spiritual heart and life circumstances that are involved in a person's deep despair and a desire to end life.

Furthermore, these biblical examples illustrate well how various motives of the heart and reactions to life's circumstances can lead to the same false gospel of suicidal thinking. What will also be observed in these case studies is that one's relationships with God and others are central to both a person's struggle and potential victory over the deceitfulness of suicidal thoughts.

4 EXAMPLES OF SUICIDAL IDEATION OR DESPAIR

Job – Job 1:1-14ff.

Job is one example of a man in the Bible who sank into deep despair. Job 3 offers a glimpse into his consideration of the value of his own life in relation to how life had traumatically unfolded against his desires and apart from his consent:

> After this Job opened his mouth and cursed the day of his birth. And Job said: "Let the day perish on which I was born, and the night that said, 'A man is conceived.' Let that day be darkness! May God above not seek it, nor light shine upon it. Let gloom and deep darkness claim it. Let clouds dwell upon it; let the blackness of the day terrify it. That night—let thick darkness seize it! Let it not rejoice among the days of the year; let it not come into the number of the months. Behold, let that night be barren; let no joyful cry enter it . . . . because it did not shut the doors of my mother's womb, nor hide trouble from my eyes. "Why did I not die at birth, come out from the womb and

expire? Why did the knees receive me? Or why
the breasts, that I should nurse? For then I
would have lain down and been quiet; I would
have slept; then I would have been at rest.

It is worth noting that while Job experienced a great many
trials in one short season of his life and his understandable
but intense despair was persistent and overwhelming, the
end of the book of Job reveals that God chose to restore
Job before he died. Yet, the text offers a glimpse into Job's
very real struggle.

Though Job clearly questioned God's sovereignty and
goodness and found himself in deep despair over the
overwhelming and seemingly unendurable suffering, he
never lost faith in God as his deliverer and restorer. In
other words, Job never placed his hope for escape from
despair in his own resources, efforts, or wisdom. Job knew
all too well that he himself could not shoulder the burdens
which he faced. Thus, while he did not fully understand
God's wisdom and divine providence, he trusted fully in
God's deliverance and mentally and physically cried out to
the Lord in deep lament.

Jonah – 4:1-4ff.

Another Old Testament figure who struggled within his
soul, pondering the value of his own life, was Jonah.

Whereas Job was "blameless and upright, one who feared God and turned away from evil" (1:1), and his traumatic circumstances were no fault of his own, Jonah's despair resulted from both his failure to obtain the deceitful desires of his flesh (selfish ambition) and his pride in not understanding his place of worship and gratitude before God.

Jonah's circumstances of discomfort and disappointment, however, did not cause his desire to die, but his physical suffering did reveal his heart's true state and struggles. When compared to Job's trials, Jonah's undesirable circumstances may not seem as grievous. Contrary to popular thinking, it is not a person's enduring intense trials/trauma that leads to suicidal ideation. Instead, it is primarily a person's internal response based upon his/her established faith within his/her likeminded community (James 1:1-8). When the trials of life come (and they always do in the post-Genesis 3 reality), they test a person's faith and reveal a person's phenomenology/ wisdom.

Jonah desired in His spiritual heart that God's wrath— rather than God's mercy—be inflicted upon the people of Nineveh. But Jonah's deceitful desires also led to his rejection of the community he should have embraced. Jonah 4:1-4 states:

> "**But it displeased Jonah exceedingly**, and he
> was angry . . . . That is why I made hast to flee

to Tarshish; for I knew that you are a gracious
God and merciful, slow to anger and abounding
in steadfast love, and relenting from disaster.
**Therefore now, O Lord, please take my life
from me, for it is better for me to die than to
live** [emphasis added]."

Clearly, Jonah's intention to die was based upon the
unfulfilled desires of his spiritual heart. Rather than
accepting God's goodness and purpose for his own life,
Jonah lost sight of that purpose and the value of life itself.

To illustrate this unfortunate and destructive human
response to not getting one's own way, the passage
records Jonah's further ideations, circumstances, and
subsequent behaviors. After being displeased by God's
mercy, Jonah isolated himself from others by going into
the outskirts of town—a common tendency for those
pursuing selfish ambitions. Proverbs 18:1 explains this
human phenomenon:

Whoever isolates himself seeks his own desire;
he breaks out against all sound judgment.

As Proverbs 8 emphasizes, rejecting God's wisdom leads to
isolation and eventually to spiritual and physical death.
Instead of being thankful to God and rejoicing with his
fellow believers, Jonah went to a hill outside the city to sit.

Though many people are likely familiar with Jonah's history, it is good to reexamine his story to see one of the heart conditions behind some suicidal ways of thinking. It is important to emphasize that Jonah does not represent all cases of suicidal thinking. But the common condition of all humanity reflected in Jonah's desires does need consideration.

Jonah 4 relates that despite Jonah's hard and selfish heart, God showed mercy to Jonah just as He had to the Ninevites. It was on the hill that God provided a gourd which offered shade to Jonah from the intense heat. Unlike God's longsuffering to the Ninevites, though, God's mercy to Jonah had brought Jonah great pleasure (6-7). But then God allowed a worm to destroy the plant and a heat wave to pass through, which left Jonah in great discomfort and displeasure (8). Jonah was in such mental distress and physical discomfort that he again expressed his heart's desire for death over life: "It is better for me to die than to live (8)." Whether a person chooses to live or to take his/her own life is decided by the treasures of the spiritual heart—often in relationship to life's circumstances. One's greatest desires always determine a person's moral decisions and subsequent behavior.

The Philippian Jailer – Acts 16:25-34

A clear example of someone who struggled with suicidal ideation and attempted to end his own life is offered in

Acts 16:25-34. Vital truths are also recorded in this passage, which provide a specific counseling framework (to be presented in the next chapter) that Paul and Silas established in helping the Philippian Jailer through his thoughts and attempted suicide. This historical account of an attempted suicide and ensuing counsel begins in verse 27:

> When the jailer woke and saw that the prison doors were open, he drew his sword and was about to kill himself, supposing that the prisoners had escaped. But Paul cried with a loud voice, "Do not harm yourself, for we are all here." And the jailer called for lights and rushed in, and trembling with fear he fell down before Paul and Silas. Then he brought them out and said, "Sirs, what must I do to be saved?" And they said, "Believe in the Lord Jesus, and you will be saved, you and your household." And they spoke the word of the Lord to him and to all who were in his house. And he took them the same hour of the night and washed their wounds; and he was baptized at once, he and all his family. Then he brought them up into his house and set food before them. And he

rejoiced along with his entire household that he
had believed in God.

The specific motives or reasons behind the jailer's thinking
were deceit, fear/anxiety, and despair (helplessness and
hopelessness). In this case, as with many suicidal
considerations, death becomes the only seemingly
available and many times desired option in the moment.
This biblical account highlights that some suicides are the
result of impulsiveness, whereas others are well-thought-
out before they are carried out. Nonetheless, deceit and
the motives of the spiritual heart underlie all non-drug
related suicides.

Paul – II Corinthians 1:8-10

As with Job and the Philippian jailer, the apostle Paul also
faced profound despair and afflictions that were beyond
his ability to shoulder. It is important to note that godly
men and women in Scripture faced incredible despair and
confessed their own inability to deal with life's mental
burdens and distressful experiences in their own strength.
As Paul expressed in 2 Corinthians 1:8-10, he wanted other
believers to be well-aware of how deep the despair was in
his own heart:

For we do not want you to be unaware,
brothers, of the affliction we experienced in

Asia. For we were so utterly burdened beyond
our strength that we despaired of life itself.
Indeed, we felt that we had received the
sentence of death. But that was to make us rely
not on ourselves but on God who raises the
dead.

Many people face insurmountable trials/traumas in life,
which they come to realize they cannot bear within their
own strength. These deeply trying experiences and the
profound struggles that follow are sometimes referred to
as the "Dark Night of the Soul."[78]

Just as the apostle Paul confessed, many Christians find
themselves with seemingly no way forward in life. While
there is no suggestion that Paul considered taking his own
life, it is evident within the context that he was mentally
tasked with thinking upon the reality of death and facing
an experience (s) beyond his own ability. When profoundly
hurtful, sorrowful, and traumatic experiences occur, it is
common for people to feel alone, to feel rejected (as Job
expressed), and to contemplate death as Paul did. But as
the Bible makes clear, this mental awareness of death is an
honest and right response to how the fallen human
condition post-Genesis 3 engages with the vexed condition

---

[78] Ronald Pies, "Psychiatry and the Dark Night of the Soul,"
Psychiatric Times (December 14, 2020): https://www.psychiatric
times.com/view/psychiatry-dark-night-soul.

of creation in general and other fallen people in particular. The problem is not thinking about death, but thinking about death apart from God's restorative wisdom and sovereign will.

The Scriptures leave no doubt that everyone should earnestly consider the inevitability of his/her own death. For example, in Ecclesiastes 7:1-4, the wise King Solomon admonishes those willing to listen to his words to be wise by solemnly considering the fact that physical death is the undeniable destiny of everyone:

> A good name is better than precious ointment, and the day of death than the day of birth. It is better to go to the house of mourning [a funeral parlor] than to go to the house of feasting [a party], for this is the end of all mankind, **and the living will lay it to heart.** Sorrow is better than laughter, for by sadness of face the heart is made glad. **The heart of the wise is in the house of mourning**, but the heart of fools is in the house of mirth [emphasis added].

Contemplating the reality of death in our spiritual hearts (and preparing for that day) is both a normal human experience and a necessary exercise of the wise. Those who think biblically about death learn to redeem their time on earth (Ephesians 5:15-17), to number their days so as to be wise (Psalm 90:12), and to have an eternal mindset and sure hope rather than a temporal focus (Titus 2:11-14; 1 Thessalonians 4:13), since both the toils and sorrows of life and the approach of death are unavoidable (Psalm 90:10). If a person naturally thinks about death apart from God's wisdom and the hope inherent in His redemptive plan, then deeper despair and destructive behavior will inevitably result.

Within the secular worldview, which alarmingly many Christians have accepted, deep despair and seemingly insurmountable distress are viewed as abnormalities and constructed into numerous psychiatric disorders. Suicidal ideation is no exception. The American Psychiatric Association believes and teaches within its faith that human distress which is profound and persistent and cannot be overcome within a person's own resources and efforts constitutes a "mental disorder."[79] When people who are deeply struggling are stigmatized ("set aside as spoiled") with a psychiatric label and categorized as abnormal, their hopelessness almost always increases. Rather than receiving help from others during a helpless state and realizing that they are not their own hope, people are told that they are disordered for their inability to resolve their own struggles and are treated accordingly.

But the apostle Paul wanted Christians to be aware of his own profound and persistent struggle so that other

---

[79] APA, *DSM-5*, 20.

Christians might be comforted in theirs. Beyond that, Paul confessed that he was weak and needed to rely on the strength of his Savior, Jesus Christ.

> Three times I pleaded with the Lord about this, that it should leave me. But he said to me, "My grace is sufficient for you, for my power is made perfect in weakness." Therefore I will boast all the more gladly of my weaknesses, so that the power of Christ may rest upon me. For the sake of Christ, then, I am content with weaknesses, insults, hardships, persecutions, and calamities. For when I am weak, then I am strong.

Paul did not pretend that he was strong and able to deliver himself from his own weakness and the very real suffering he experienced in this life. Instead, he placed his dependence upon God. As Scripture teaches, unbearable human suffering and persistent despair are expected phenomena to be experienced in humanity's fallen condition. Yet, this biblical way of thinking is antithetical to humanistic teaching so prevalent in today's society.

Whatever trial/burden a person faces, he/she must either rely upon human wisdom to establish hope and strength or follow in the steps of Paul and by faith depend upon God who not only can sustain a person's life but who raises people from the dead. But Scripture makes it clear that human wisdom cannot deliver humanity's soul from its deepest troubles—whether humanly or naturally caused). Psalm 60:11 and 108:12 express this important truth in a prayer to God: "Give us help from trouble, for the help of man is useless" (KJV). The person/object of hope that is established by faith (Romans 12:1) determines whether a person in despair can go forward positively in life or will turn to hopes that are doomed to fail. Stated otherwise, going through deep traumas or being weak does not determine that people will commit suicide. Nonetheless, one's faith/identity in relationship to God and others and his/her heart's desires/values ultimately determine one's responses in life.

Unlike the apostle Paul, who in his weakness turned to and depended upon Christ, many suicide attempts and completions represent the last entry in a person's failed list of attempts to establish hope in self, other people, things, and/or experiences which he/she deceitfully believes offers satisfaction and deliverance. Contemplating the reality of one's own death is neither a sickness nor a sin; it is thinking honestly about the human condition and the inevitable experience that awaits. But one's faith in how he/she views God, life and death, his/her own self, and others, will inevitably shape that person's moral behaviors. These are all issues that establish the necessity for biblical phenomenology.

4 EXAMPLES OF SUICIDAL COMPLETIONS

In addition to examples of individuals who struggled in deep despair, Scripture offers many examples of people who not only contemplated suicide but also acted upon their thoughts and desires. An examination of four of those cases is beneficial to better understand how different motives undergird suicidal thinking.

Ahithophel - 2 Samuel 17:20-23

The life and death of Ahithophel, counselor to King David, reveals how both a person's life history (and their responses) and his/her spiritual heart processes are major factors in why people choose to take their own lives. 2 Samuel 17:20-23 relates the history of Ahithophel:

> Moreover, Ahithophel said to Absalom, "Let me choose twelve thousand men, and I will arise and pursue David tonight. And I will bring all the people back to you as a bride comes home to her husband. You seek the life of only one man, and all the people will be at peace." And the advice seemed right in the eyes of Absalom and all the elders of Israel . . . . When Absalom's servants came to the woman at the house, they

said, "Where are Ahimaaz and Jonathan?" And the woman said to them, "They have gone over the brook of water." And when they had sought and could not find them, they returned to Jerusalem. After they had gone, the men came up out of the well, and went and told King David. They said to David, "Arise, and go quickly over the water, for thus and so has Ahithophel counseled against you." Then David arose, and all the people who were with him, and they crossed the Jordan. By daybreak not one was left who had not crossed the Jordan. **When Ahithophel saw that his advice had not been followed**, he saddled his donkey and set out for his house in his hometown. **He put his house in order and then hanged himself. So he died and was buried in his father's tomb** [emphasis added].

When Ahithophel realized that he would not have his desires fulfilled and his will would not prevail, he carefully arranged the taking of his own life. As with other biblical figures, Ahithophel illustrates how some people who attempt suicide do so thoughtfully, whereas others do so impulsively. The motive behind Ahithophel's suicide was the combination of guilt, fear, disappointment, and poor relationships.

Zimri – 1 Kings 16:9-20

King Zimri represents a similar case to that of Ahithophel, since both men's histories included betrayal and attempted murder. 1 Kings 16:15-20 recounts,

> But his servant Zimri, commander of half his chariots, conspired against him. When he was at Tirzah, drinking himself drunk in the house of Arza, who was over the household in Tirzah, Zimri came in and struck him down and killed him, in the twenty-seventh year of Asa king of Judah, and reigned in his place . . . . In the twenty-seventh year of Asa king of Judah, Zimri reigned seven days in Tirzah. Now the troops were encamped against Gibbethon, which belonged to the Philistines, and the troops who were encamped heard it said, "Zimri has conspired, and he has killed the king." Therefore all Israel made Omri, the commander of the army, king over Israel that day in the camp. So Omri went up from Gibbethon, and all Israel with him, and they besieged Tirzah. **And when Zimri saw that the city was taken, he went into the citadel of the king's house and**

burned the king's house over him with fire and died, because of his sins that he committed, doing evil in the sight of the LORD, walking in the way of Jeroboam, and for his sin which he committed, making Israel to sin. Now the rest of the acts of Zimri, and the conspiracy that he made, are they not written in the Book of the Chronicles of the Kings of Israel [emphasis added]?

When Zimri realized that his many sins had caught up with him and that his desire to be King would not be fulfilled, he decided that the control of his own fate rather than repentance was of utmost importance to him. Just as with self-harm (cutting, bulimia, anorexia, etc.), control is often at the center of suicidal ideation and attempts, as such extreme behavior is usually sourced in the recognition that not only a person's current life is out of control but also subsequent attempts to control whatever aspects of life that person believes he/she should control will fail. Zimri's specific motive in taking his own life is provided in the text. Twice the passage pronounces that it was "because of the sins which he committed." The sense of being unable to atone for one's sin, resolve the guilt, and remedy the despair influence some people to consider or complete suicide.

Samson – Judges 16:23-31

Samson is another person recorded in Scripture whose spiritual heart and moral history reveal his arrival at a mental state that perceived the taking of his own life to be a desirable outcome. After forsaking the commands of God by following the desires of his own heart and being betrayed by those who he falsely believed loved him, Samson found himself imprisoned by his enemies:

> Now the lords of the Philistines gathered to offer a great sacrifice to Dagon their god and to rejoice, and they said, "Our god has given Samson our enemy into our hand." And when the people saw him, they praised their god. For they said, "Our god has given our enemy into our hand, the ravager of our country, who has killed many of us." And when their hearts were merry, they said, "Call Samson, that he may entertain us." So they called Samson out of the prison, and he entertained them. They made him stand between the pillars. And Samson said to the young man who held him by the hand, "Let me feel the pillars on which the house rests, that I may lean against them." Now the house was full of men and women. All the lords

of the Philistines were there, and on the roof there were about 3,000 men and women, who looked on while Samson entertained. Then Samson called to the LORD and said, "O Lord GOD, please remember me and please strengthen me only this once, O God, **that I may be avenged on the Philistines for my two eyes**." And Samson grasped the two middle pillars on which the house rested, and he leaned his weight against them, his right hand on the one and his left hand on the other. **And Samson said, "Let me die with the Philistines." Then he bowed with all his strength, and the house fell upon the lords and upon all the people who were in it. So the dead whom he killed at his death were more than those whom he had killed during his life.** Then his brothers and all his family came down and took him and brought him up and buried him between Zorah and Eshtaol in the tomb of Manoah his father. He had judged Israel twenty years [emphasis added].

Samson's desire to avenge his enemies—those who had blinded him—became greater than his desire to live. As with most suicide attempts and completions, the greatest desire/treasure of the heart will always guide a person's thinking and outworking behavior. Whereas Samson's motive is clearly expressed as vengeance in the context of this biblical narrative, it is not always so easy to discern in suicide attempts and completions.

It is also worth noting from this passage of Scripture that God did grant Samson his request of returned strength. But God did not encourage or command Samson to sacrifice his own life. Instead, Samson's actions were based upon his own motives and desires. It is entirely probable that God would have returned not only Samson's strength but also his sight and freedom had he asked. But according to the text, Samson was focused on his own revenge.

Judas – Matthew 27:3-5

Likely the most well-known of all cases of suicidal completions recorded in Scripture is that of Judas the Iscariot:

> Then when Judas, his betrayer, saw that Jesus
> was condemned, he changed his mind and
> brought back the thirty pieces of silver to the
> chief priests and the elders, saying, "I have
> sinned by betraying innocent blood." They said,
> "What is that to us? See to it yourself." And

throwing down the pieces of silver into the
temple, he departed, and he went and hanged
himself.

Here Judas partially repents of his deceitful desires of the
flesh. But unlike the criminal who died by Jesus' side while
on the cross, Judas did not seek Christ's forgiveness, nor
did he make any effort to restore broken relationships.
The metaphysical reality of moral guilt and the spiritual
trauma of broken relationships are usually extremely
heavy burdens to bear in the soul.

Although the Bible stresses the destructive results of
attempting to appease one's own guilt and cover one's
own sins, secularists are also beginning to realize the
destructive nature to the soul that one's moral failures and
subsequent unresolved guilt can have:

> **Moral integrity represents the depth of an**
> **individual's inner core**, not a simple dichotomy
> of right and wrong. As such, when a person's
> moral integrity is jeopardized in some fashion,
> **they lose touch with their inner identity**. It may
> lead to overestimating or disowning personal
> agency as a protection against the aloneness
> and helplessness inherent in triage-limited
> decision-making. As a result, **many of the**
> **components of posttraumatic suffering and**

chronic grief (such as guilt, remorse, shame, or considering oneself infallible) are experienced in a far deeper way, since the sense of meaning and existence are in jeopardy. Denial of uncertainty, compartmentalizing helplessness, and experiencing life-long anticipatory mourning are possible consequences. And when resilience is necessary, an inability to grieve helplessness and vulnerability can lead to culturally sanctioned, socially toxic prejudices. Individuals suffering from moral injuries are different from those who are not. Moral injury means that an individual's self-definition is on the line. Efforts to mitigate their post-traumatic spectrum symptoms may only provide partial remedy for their problems. Individuals suffering greatly may become angry, blaming caregivers, **in an effort to retain an illusion of control. They**

frequently experience feelings of doom greater than depression [emphasis added].[80]

An awareness of death/doom/condemnation, deep sorrow, and despair (hopelessness and helplessness) are all born out of humanity's moral nature, and guilt is a very real and necessary phenomenon of the soul post-Genesis 3.

Both the deceitful desires of the flesh and the resulting traumatic guilt that naturally occurs when God's moral law—written on the hearts of mankind (Romans 2)—is violated in a way that a person's phenomenology/identity is greatly damaged can be observed in the life of Judas. Sin and guilt, if they are not properly brought into moral balance and appeased, are incredibly destructive and lead to a state of hopelessness and despair and potentially to self-flagellation/harm.[81]

Many secular studies, such as published in *JAMA Psychiatry,* highlight how both guilt and selfishness

---

[80] Terry R. Bard and Harold J. Bursztajn, "Triage Trauma and Moral Distress," *Psychiatric Times* (October 1, 2020): https://www.psychiatrictimes.com/view/triage-trauma-moral-distress?utm_source=sfmc%E2%80%8B&utm_medium=email%E2%80%8B&utm_campaign=10022020_UNSPONSORED_PT_eNL%E2%80%8B%E2%80%8B&eKey=ZHJiZXJnZXIuZHJAZ21haWwuY29t.

[81] Ibid.

explained within the secular construct of Borderline Personality Disorder (BPD) lead to a poor phenomenology/ personal identity and many times to suicidal attempts. The selfish and isolating mentality and behaviors described in the BPD construct result in guilt and contribute to shaping one's negative view of self. As the study also reveals, being self-focused and antisocial naturally leads to being anxious over abandonment and further rejection:

> specific criteria of identity disturbance, chronic feelings of emptiness, and frantic efforts to avoid abandonment emerged as significant factors associated with prospectively observed suicide attempt status.[82]

Broken relationships, identity, guilt, despair, selfishness, unfulfilled desires, and anxiety are all motives recorded in Scripture as suicidal ideations.

Based upon the Scriptural case studies offered here (and others), it becomes clear that many people do not choose the circumstances that lead them into a mental state of deep despair and the consideration of death. Still,

---

[82] Shirley Yen, Jessica R. Peters, Shivani Nishar, et al., "Association of Borderline Personality Disorder Criteria with Suicide Attempts: Findings From the Collaborative Longitudinal Study of Personality Disorders Over 10 Years of Follow-up," *JAMA Psychiatry* vol. 78 (2) (November 18, 2020): 187–194; doi:10.1001/jamapsychiatry.2020.3598.

considering suicide as a viable option rests both in the individual's own phenomenology and morality and in the influential people that surround him/her.

Moreover, many of the individuals in case studies examined from Scripture who both contemplated death and eventually took their own lives already had an established pattern of deceitful and selfish thinking in their hearts and a history of moral failures, fears, and guilt which they attempted to deal with on their own. Their own selfish choices led them to further selfish decisions and seemingly insurmountable guilt. Within their own deceived thinking apart from the truth of Christ that sets humanity free, they found no way forward in life. In these cases, the consideration of suicide as a legitimate form of deliverance was a thought process that increased over time through many sinful choices and from many broken relationships.

In the instances of Ahithophel, Zimri, and Judas, each of them had attempted to or had betrayed a king—a moral crime in their day that would have surely resulted in the death penalty. Even so, in these three biblical case studies, the correlate to suicide is not so much betrayal as it is idolatry (misplaced desires) and subsequent guilt. All three of these men were willing to kill themselves or to have another killed to fulfill their own desires and maintain the false belief that they were in control of their own destinies. In other words, selfish ambition and the corresponding guilt and anxiety/fear were the driving forces of their lives prior to their suicidal completions. Each of these men wanted something so badly that the value of life (including the lives of others) became secondary to the fulfillment of selfish desires (James 4:1-4).

Whether people enter a season of despair and believe that death is imminent, or they are pursuing deceitful desires, all are responsible for their own reactions to life's heavy burdens and deferred hopes. Furthermore, people are ultimately responsible to choose a person or object of hope in which they place their faith. This selected hope is always based upon their hearts' treasures and will determine whether they find deliverance or digress further into destructive behavior that leads to death.

CHAPTER 9

HOPE STILL EXISTS

Because suicidal ideation most often represents a false hope of deliverance, deep-seated deceit, and poor or broken relationships, establishing God's perspective and genuine hope in Christ is of the highest priority in helping others to deny the false gospel of suicide. In contrast to the secular teaching of bio-determinism, a person's suicidal ideation is not the end of his/her life or an indication that suicidal thinking will persist. As many secularists acknowledge, most cases of suicidal thinking are temporary.[83] In fact, it is estimated that 9 out of 10 people who attempt suicide and survive never do so again.[84] If destructive motives, deceitful desires, poor relationships, self-focus, perspectives on life, and the negative effects of psychotropic drugs are not identified and addressed truthfully and lovingly, however, the

---

[83] Kristen Fuller, "5 Common Myths about Suicide Debunked," *NAMI* (September 30, 2020): https://www.nami.org/Blogs/NAMI-Blog/September-2020/5-Common-Myths-About-Suicide-Debunked.

[84] Matthew Miller and David Hemenway, "Guns and Suicide in the United States," *NEJM* vol. 359 (September 4, 2008): 989-91; https://www.nejm.org/doi/full/10.1056/NEJMp0805923.

consideration of suicide may persist throughout the remainder of a person's life.

Countless people who have either come to realize the deceitful and destructive nature of their own suicidal ideation or survived their own suicide attempt bear witness to the fact that a purposeful and meaningful life begins when they embrace truth that sets them free, provides a means of obtaining healthy relationships, and establishes a sure hope. These are individuals who in hindsight express sincere regret for their delusional thinking which led them to attempt taking their own lives.[85] The only genuine and lasting hope for resolving the dark deep waters of suicide is the living water, Jesus Christ, who sets the captives free.

APPROACHING THOSE IN DESPAIR

In addition to numerous case studies, the Bible also records practical wisdom for Christians who desire to offer life-changing hope to those in deep despair. Paul's counseling of the Philippian jailer, recorded in Acts 16:25-

---

[85] E.g., The stories of Ken Hines and Ken Baldwin, "Second Chances: 'I survived jumping off the Golden Gate Bridge," *ABC 7 News* (May 18, 2017): https://abc7news. com/society/second-chances-i-survived-jumping-off-the-golden-gate-bridge/2010562/.

34, offers pastors, parents, biblical counselors, and other helpers both a model of counseling procedures to follow when an individual is contemplating suicide and genuine hope that is vital to resolving suicidal ideation.

It is beneficial, then, to revisit Acts 16 and carefully examine Paul's counsel to the Philippian jailer. In this text one can observe five important aspects of biblical counseling:

> When the jailer woke and saw that the prison
> doors were open, he drew his sword and was
> about to kill himself, supposing that the
> prisoners had escaped. **[1]** But Paul cried with a
> loud voice, "Do not harm yourself, **[2-3]** for we
> are all here." And the jailer called for lights and
> rushed in, and trembling with fear **[4]** he fell
> down before Paul and Silas. Then he brought
> them out and said, "Sirs, what must I do to be
> saved?" **[5]** And they said, "Believe in the Lord
> Jesus, and you will be saved, you and your
> household." And they spoke the word of the
> Lord to him and to all who were in his house.
> And he took them the same hour of the night
> and washed their wounds; and he was baptized
> at once, he and all his family. Then he brought
> them up into his house and set food before

them. And he rejoiced along with his entire
household that he had believed in God.

If Paul and Silas had not offered the Philippian jailer
comfort and counsel in his time of crisis, it is likely that the
jailer would have taken his own life that day. Acts 16
provides counselors with the necessary procedures in
approaching those with suicidal ideation, those who are
on the verge of a suicidal attempt, or those who have
failed at an attempted suicide.

1. Communicate Genuine Care

These elements of biblical counseling are important to
identify, but they were all applied within a loving
relationship. Discussed previously and reiterated in this
text is the reality that compassion within meaningful
relationships is vital to nurture human life in general and
specifically to help people through suicidal ideations.
Compassion and comfort are crucial, since they establish
worth, wisdom, identity, and a direction in life toward
which to head. When life loses value or meaning, as it
often does with the loss of relationships or through the
involvement in relationships that are toxic, death can
easily become a person's greatest desire.

Every beneficial counseling situation must be viewed and
approached through the biblical lens of relationships,
which requires that love for God and others be the

foundation (Matthew 22:36-40). When biblical compassion/empathy and biblical truth guide counseling, either discipleship or evangelism are inevitably occurring.

It is also helpful to revisit 2 Corinthians 1:3-9 to see clearly not only Paul's high priority in caring for others he counseled but also the basis of his compassion/empathy. Just as he did with the Philippian jailer, Paul began his counsel to the believers at Corinth (who were also under heavy persecution and themselves in despair) by first presenting a theology of comfort and compassion:

> Blessed be the God and Father of our Lord Jesus Christ, the **Father of mercies** [compassion] and **God of all comfort, who comforts us in all our affliction, so that we may be able to comfort those who are in any affliction, with the comfort with which we ourselves are comforted by God** . . . . For we do not want you to be unaware, brothers, of the affliction we experienced in Asia. For we were so utterly burdened beyond our strength that we despaired of life itself. Indeed, we felt that we had received the sentence of death. But that was to make us rely not on ourselves but on God who raises the dead [emphasis added].

Paul rightly understood that he could not effectively counsel those in despair until he himself knew intimately the God of compassion and comfort, which is why pointing others to Christ was of the highest priority.

Paul also used his own personal struggles as an example so that those who were in mental distress and suffering could identify with him and hear his words. In the same way, when biblical counselors share their own fragility with counselees and give testimony of being comforted and finding life and hope in the giver of life and the God of hope, the counselors establish meaningful relationships and turn the hearers toward the only true Deliverer. In essence, they offer to those willing to listen empirical evidence (a testimony) that they themselves have a good Savior who is fully sufficient to deliver hurting and broken people from the darkest struggles and give them an abundant life.

Secularists have also come to realize through extensive research that one of the most influential factors of positive change within counseling is empathy—what is referred to as the "therapeutic alliance":

> The therapeutic alliance is taught and commonly regarded as essential in engendering change. The formation and maintenance of such an alliance often involves the corrective emotional experience of the patient with the

therapist and **the therapist's ability to relate empathetically . . . . It is a common conclusion in the psychotherapy literature that the therapeutic alliance accounts for a significant part of the variance in client change.** In a review of the impact of the therapeutic alliance, the following four elements were identified as composing the therapeutic alliance: (i) the patient's capacity to work purposefully, (ii) the patient's affective bond to the therapist, (iii) the therapist's empathic understanding and involvement, and (iv) agreement about the goals and tasks of treatment. This review of the research led to the conclusion that "the alliance may be even more central to change than initially thought" [emphasis added].[86]

Though unbelievers can display aspects of God's character—such as comfort and empathy—without acknowledging that mankind is created in the image of God who is love and provides life, leading people into

---

[86] Virginia A. Galloway and Stanley L. Brodsky, "Caring Less, Doing More: The Role of Therapeutic Detachment with Volatile and Unmotivated Clients," *American Journal of Psychotherapy* vol. 57 (1) (2003): 32; https://psychotherapy.psychiatryonline. org/doi/pdf/10.1176/appi.psychotherapy.2003.57.1.32.

genuine hope through empathy, as Paul offered, cannot be accomplished apart from God's grace. Therefore, it is not enough to be empathetic and to comfort others in human effort, though any compassion and comfort reflects the moral law of God the Creator (Matthew 22:36-40) that is written on every human heart (Romans 2:12-16) and which will certainly be of benefit to others. Human compassion and comfort are healing because they imperfectly manifest God's good character that leads people to positively change their minds (Romans 2:4).

When Paul realized that the Philippian jailer was in a state of mental crisis, Paul did not initially preach the gospel to him. Instead, the Apostle Paul displayed the compassion and comfort of the Savior that he knew so well. Paul's compassion for the jailer who was contemplating the value of his life opened the door to the eventual opportunity for Paul to offer the jailer eternal life. According to a well-known adage, "No one cares how much you know until they know how much you care." Like Paul's interaction with the jailor, the presentation of the gospel must be relational and sourced in God's love.

The Philippian jailer had likely observed the beatings and suffering of Paul and Silas and knew well that these men faced a death sentence for their faith in God. When they chose to help him rather than to help themselves escape, compassion was clearly demonstrated from Paul and Silas to the jailer.

In most cases, compassion is most easily displayed in simply being with the one who is struggling and sincerely listening to that person's struggles. Giving to others one's time and attention not only conveys the value of that person's life but also safeguards against further isolation that can lead to a suicidal attempt. Many suicide survivors offer testimony that if just one person would have shown interest in their lives or interacted with them in a caring way, they would have changed their minds about the potential of taking their own lives.[87]

2. Discern the Heart's Motives

After Paul shows the jailer compassion and comforts him, he then discerns what is motiving the jailer to take his own life. In the case of the jailer, his actions were driven by fear/anxiety, and Paul confronted this ideation in a gracious but clear manner. It is important to emphasize that although Paul was able to quickly discern the deep waters within the jailer's spiritual heart, it often takes much longer for a person to reveal the source/motive underlying the dark consideration of suicide. The events of Acts 16 unfold within a short period of time, but this is not always the case. Sometimes the individual's words reveal

---

[87] E.g., The stories of Ken Hines and Ken Baldwin, "Second Chances: 'I survived jumping off the Golden Gate Bridge," *ABC 7 News* (May 18, 2017): https://abc7news. com/society/second-chances-i-survived-jumping-off-the-golden-gate-bridge/2010562/.

his/her spiritual heart, while at other times a loved one or counselor is only able to discern the content of the spiritual heart from his/her being involved in that person's life over time. Nonetheless, discerning what a person's foundational struggles are goes deeper than the current crisis, and establishing a multitude of counselors who are involved in discerning the heart is wise (Proverbs 11:14; 24:6b).

As observed in the biblical case studies discussed in the previous chapter, there are numerous motives that can exist within a person's soul and which can lead to suicidal attempts. These purposes/motives are what counselors should seek to discover: (1) selfish ambition, (2) anxiety/fear, (3) revenge, (4) deceitful desires of the flesh, (5) guilt, (6) broken relationships, (7) deep sorrow, and (8) false hopes/crushed spirit/despair. Not all motives behind suicidal ideation and attempts are the same, and thus a good counselor will discern the deep waters of each person's soul (Proverbs 20:5).

In cases of suicidal thinking where psychotropic drugs are involved, parents and counselors should seek out a like-minded physician who is knowledgeable about conditions such as *akathisia, tardive dyskinesia, tardive dysphoria, drug withdrawal syndrome*, suicidal ideation, and the numerous other impairing effects so often produced by psychiatric drugs. Counselors should kindly share the clear published empirical data, lovingly explain how these drugs regularly induce suicidal thoughts, and if knowledgeable, offer insight into how these chemicals produce many troubling physical conditions which explain a counselee's symptoms. Since many consumers are unaware that suicidal ideation regularly increases through the consumption of these prescribed drugs, walking families through the FDA's warning labels and manufacturers' published "side-effects" for specific drugs is often beneficial.

It must be made clear, though, that counselors should never advise others to begin or end taking psychotropic drugs. Non-licensed individuals can and should offer published evidence about prescription drugs and encourage families to do extensive research to better facilitate a discerning choice. But counselors/helpers should never offer medical advice. The individual and/or the guardians must themselves decide whether the drugs are influencing suicidal ideation, whether the individual wishes to continue consuming them, and whether he/she desires to work with a competent physician to deprescribe them. Still, the understandable need to escape the often-torturous effects of psychotropics drugs must be considered as a possible motive underlying many people's suicidal thoughts.

3. Confront the Underlying Deceit

While the purposes of the heart may vary between cases, deceitful thinking is a central feature of all suicidal thinking. In every suicidal thought and attempt, the false hope exists that by ending one's life, a person can find spiritual life, satisfaction, and/or deliverance. Many people who find themselves in despair and struggle in deep sorrow also erroneously believe that despair ceases when their lives end. But sorrow and despair do not end with suicide; they are transferred to those who survive. Sorrow and despair will not be resolved until genuine hope in Christ is fully realized (Revelation 21:3-4; 26;12).

In addition to the false hope of deliverance, there are often other forms of deceit that lead people toward death. In the case of the Philippian jailer, he falsely believed that Paul and Silas had escaped. Because the jailer's deceitful thinking also led to his anxiety/fear, Paul quickly confronted these issues.

In other cases, it is the deceitfulness of pride (Proverbs 16:18-19) and the deceitful desires of the flesh (Ephesians 4:21-25ff.) which lead to the soul's destruction. Pride is another deep deceit that counselors must compassionately explore and graciously address. The example of Abimelech in Judges 9:52-54, who died via *suicide by proxy*,[88] illustrates how pride in the heart can sometimes lead to death. If a person is driven by selfish ambition and pride, then the natural way that seems right

---

[88] *Suicide by proxy* is a term used to describe those who wish to die but are unable to take their own lives. These people find ways to have others carry out the act for them.

in one's own perspective, rather than the mind of Christ, is guiding the heart (Philippians 2:1-5).

Certainly, every deceived soul needs to find identity, purpose, deliverance, and meaning within a covenant relationship with Christ. Stated otherwise, all people need to be restored to life as God designed it to be before the fall of Adam and, thereafter, abide in His truth.

4. Address Relationships Involved

The Jailer's fear/anxiety was born out of a deceitful assumption, but his internal struggle reflected his relationships with both his authority and with Paul and Silas. In this case, Paul and Silas were able to resolve the relational problems in which they were involved (they had not escaped as the jailer falsely believed), and the jailer's fear of death from failing his superiors ceased. Most crisis counseling, though, involves people who intervene at some point after the suicidal individual's relationship problems have escalated but who are not present to work out relational problems immediately as they occur.

In every case of suicidal ideation, attempts, and completions recorded in Scripture, broken or sinful relationships are present. Counselors are wise to contemplate and discover what broken, inappropriate, and/or influential relationships are impacting a person's consideration of suicide. Some relationships will need to be restored while others will need to be discontinued in a biblical manner by the one who is struggling.

As Paul and Silas wisely did, making sure that the most important relationship with Jesus Christ exists in the counselee's heart is of vital importance. Biblical counselors do not merely seek to save temporal lives—though certainly that is a valid and urgent concern. Prompting eternal life with Christ is always the predominant perspective when wise counsel is offered to those in despair and contemplating suicide.

5. Offer the "Anchor of the Soul"

What people—especially those who are in deep despair and are desiring to act upon deceitful thinking—need most is to hear the comforting, truthful, and hope-filled Word of God. When people are deceived into thinking that they must deliver themselves and that physical death becomes their most attractive option of escape, suicide then seems to be the most rational choice.

But Paul and Silas offered the Philippian jailer an alternative way to view not only himself and his circumstances but also life in general. Central to their counsel was "the Word of the Lord," which is "the discerner of the thoughts and intents of the heart" (Hebrews 4:12). The Bible offers both life-giving hope for the one struggling and necessary discernment for the those who are counseling. If a person is struggling with suicidal thoughts, then accurately answering "why" they are struggling is essential. If the question of "why" someone has arrived at a desire to take his/her life is to be answered accurately, though, the Word of God must be both graciously offered and applied.

What the human soul needs—especially in a time of crisis—is a sure anchor for the soul. While false hopes may help for a time, they always result in deeper despair and death. Scripture alone offers the only genuine hope available to the soul in need. Hebrews 6:17-20 explains,

> So when God desired to show more convincingly to the heirs of the promise the unchangeable character of his purpose, he guaranteed it with an oath, so that by two unchangeable things, in which it **is impossible for God to lie, we who have fled for refuge might have strong encouragement to hold fast to the hope set before us. We have this as a sure and steadfast anchor of the soul, a hope that enters into the inner place behind the curtain, where Jesus has gone as a forerunner on our behalf,** having become a high priest forever after the order of Melchizedek.

While no one can prevent other people from carrying out their own suicides, there is genuine hope for those who are struggling in their thoughts and who desire help. Essentially, a person's faith, desires, and relationships determine his/her pursuits, behavior, and future. If a person in need does not desire to be helped, then those who long to bear the burden of the one struggling cannot manipulate a change of heart and rescue that person out of his/her despair. All they can do is compassionately comfort, graciously confront, diligently pray for the one in need, and consistently offer him/her gospel hope that alone can deliver anyone in mental turmoil from any vexation of the soul.

If suicidal ideation represents misplaced desires, unhealthy relationships, and a delusional way of thinking about oneself and the life that God has gifted to each person, then only God's truth—a biblical phenomenology/ wisdom— within a covenant relationship with Him can set a person free. False hope must be replaced with genuine hope, and life-changing hope is a supernatural gift of the Holy Spirit received only through the hearing of the Word of God (Romans 15:13).

CONCLUSION

Suicidal ideation is a disturbing perversion of the gospel of Jesus Christ. It is a deceitful faith and destructive desire which insists that taking one's physical life brings about a fulfilled spiritual life; that by taking one's life, love is offered to others; that laying down one's life for one's self produces joy and remedies despair; that salvation is leaning unto one's own understanding and internal resources; that guilt can be dealt with by one's own atonement for sins; that relationships can be mended through death; and that deep sorrow can end by taking one's own life. Suicidal ideation is a false gospel which insists that rather than living as a sacrifice unto God in reasonable worship (Romans 12:1-3), one should die in idolatry in an effort to discover life.

Pastors, biblical counselors, Christian parents, Christian teachers, and Christian medical personnel are all equipped with grace and truth that can perfectly deliver the human soul from the deep dark waters of deceitful thinking that leads to death. But only those who desire help will receive the living water of the Word, and just as with the Philippian jailer, when God's grace is received, true life follows.

Though most people earnestly desire to see their loved ones and others experience life abundantly, it is only through the ministry of the Holy Spirit that genuine hope can be established in the soul. Those who have a covenant relationship with Christ are responsible and privileged to offer this life-giving hope to those in need and to pray for a counselee's change of mind, while gratefully acknowledging that new life in Christ is the gift of the Holy Spirit effectively working through the living Word of God. This reality makes prayer—the counselor's dependence upon God's work—a vital aspect of all counseling. Where deceit exists, there is always spiritual warfare.

Because of the depraved nature of the spiritual heart and the fallen world, the problem of suicide will not go away until God makes all things new. This truth demands that every helper both establish a way to best approach those struggling and to be equipped and competent to counsel. A counselor may choose to continue trusting in the failed humanistic bio-psycho-social model or decisively accept biblical wisdom concerning the same human phenomena. Yet, the fact remains that faith and wisdom guide every counselor/helper in approaching people with suicidal ideations.

There is still hope for those in desperate need, who find themselves in the deepest and darkest waters of despair and deceit. But this unique faith and hope is in the living water of God found only in Christ Jesus as recorded in the all-sufficient Word of God.

BIBLIOGRAPHY

American Psychiatric Association. *Diagnostic and Statistical Manual of Mental Disorders*. 5th ed. Washington, DC: American Psychiatric Publishing, 2013.

———. *"DSM-5* Table of Contents," Downloadable PDF: https://www. google.com/url?sa =t&rct=j&q=& esrc=s&source =web&cd=&ved=2ahUKEwj8_dXYlK 3sAhXhnuAKHd-fAqgQFjABegQIAxAC&url=https% 3A%2F%2F www.psychiatry.org%2FFile%2520 Library%2FPsychiatrists%2FPractice%2FDSM%2FAP A_DSM-5-Contents.pdf&usg=AOvVaw3Mt3AhQ08d Loi9pctYxvj6.

Anderson, Pauline. "Celebrity Suicides Trigger Copycat Deaths by Same Method," *Medscape Psychiatry* (May 10, 2018): https://www.medscape.com/view article/896452#vp_2.

Atbasoglu, E. Cem. Schultz, Susan K. and Andreasen, Nancy C. "the Relationship of Akathisia with Suicidality and Depersonalization among Patients with Schizophrenia," *The Journal of Neuropsychiatry and Clinical Neurosciences vol. 13 (3)* (August 1, 2001): 336; see also https://doi.org/10.1176/jnp.13.3.336.

Bard, Terry and Bursztajn, Harold J. "Triage Trauma and Moral Distress," *Psychiatric Times* (October 1, 2020): https://www.psychiatrictimes.com/view/triage-trauma-moral-distress?utm_source=sfmc%E2%80%8B&utm_medium=email%E2%80%8B&utm_campaign=10022020_UNSPONSORED_PT_eNL%E2%80%8B%E2%80%8B&eKey=ZHJiZXJnZXIuZHJAZ21haWwuY29t.

Brauser, Deborah. "Is Patient Suicide in Psychiatry a 'Medical Error'? *Medscape Psychiatry* (October 14, 2020): https://www.medscape.com/viewarticle/939130?nlid=137853_2051&src=WNL_mdplsnews_201016_mscpedit_psyc&uac=264124BV&spon=12&impID=2623271&faf=1.

Brauser, Deborah. "US Suicides Increasing at 'Alarming Rate," Says CDC," *Medscape Psychiatry* (June 7, 2018): https://www.medscape.com/viewarticle/897804.

Berger II, Daniel R. *The Chemical Imbalance Delusion*. Taylors, SC: Alethia International Publications, 2019.

———. *Rethinking Depression: Not a Sickness, Not a Sin*. Taylors, SC: Alethia International Publications, 2019.

—————. *Saving Abnormal: The Disorder of Psychiatric Genetics*. Taylors, SC: Alethia International Publications, 2020.

Bernert, Rebecca A, and Thomas E Joiner. "Sleep disturbances and suicide risk: A review of the literature." *Neuropsychiatric disease and treatment* vol. 3,6 (2007): 735-43. doi:10.2147/ndt.s1248.

Breggin, Peter R. *Toxic Psychiatry*. New York: St. Martin's Press, 1991.

Brooks, Megan. "Sleep Loss Unleashes Anger," *Medscape Psychiatry* (September 15, 2020): https://www.medscape.com /viewarticle/937414?nlid=137426_2051&src=WNL_mdplsnews_ 200918_mscpedit_psyc&uac= 264124BV&spon=12&impID=2572773&faf=1.

Burne, Jerome. "Could Antidepressants really cause brain damage? Experts reveal the pills don't work for most people and could even cause PERMANENT harm," *Daily Mail Online* (February 6, 2017): https://www.dailymail.co.uk/health/article-4197460/Could-antidepressants-damage-brain.html.

Burns, Wendy. "Wendy Burns: Medical Community must ensure that those needing support to come off antidepressants can get it," *The British Medical*

Journal (September 25, 2020): https://blogs.bmj. com/bmj/2020/09/25/wendy-burn-medical-community-must-ensure-that-those-needing-support-to-come-off-anti-depressants-can-get-it/.

Carpiniello, Bernardo and Pinna, Federica. "The Reciprocal Relationship between Suicidality and Stigma," *Frontiers in Psychiatry* vol. 8 (35) (March 8, 2017): doi:10.3389/fpsyt.2017.00035.

Crick, Francis, Skinner, B.F., and Greening, Thomas, et. al. *Humanist Manifestos I and II* edited by Paul Kurtz. Buffalo, NY: Prometheus Books, 1973.

Conroy, J. Oliver. "An apocalyptic cult, 900 dead: remembering the Jonestown massacre, 40 years on," *The Guardian* (November 17, 2018): https://www.theguardian. com/world/2018/nov /17/an-apocalyptic-cult-900-dead-remembering-the-jonestown-massacre-40-years-on.

Dreier, Mareike, Ludwig, Julia, Härter, Martin, von dem Knesebeck, Olaf, Baumgardt, Johanna, Bock, Thomas, Dirmaier, Jorg, Kennedy, Alison J., Brumby, Susan A. and Liebherz, Sarah. "Development and evaluation of e-mental health interventions to reduce stigmatization of suicidality - a study protocol," *BMC Psychiatry* vol. 19 (1): (May 17, 2019): 152. doi: 10.1186/s12888-019-2137-0. PMID: 31101103; PMCID: PMC6525463.

Fried, Stephen. Rush: Revolution, Madness, and the
Visionary Doctor who became a Founding Father
1st edition. NY: Random House, 2018.

Galloway, Virginia A. and Brodsky, Stanley L. "Caring Less,
Doing More: The Role of Therapeutic Detachment
with Volatile and Unmotivated Clients," *American
Journal of Psychotherapy* vol. 57 (1) (2003): 32;
https://psychotherapy.psychiatryonline. org/doi/
pdf/10.1176/appi.psychotherapy.2003.57.1.32.

Gardner, Caleb and Kleinman, Arthur. "Medicine and the
Mind-The Consequences of Psychiatry's Identity
Crisis," *New England Journal of Medicine* (October
31, 2019): https://doi.org/10.1056/nejmp1910603.

Healy, David and Aldred, Graham. "Antidepressant Drug
Use and the Risk of Suicide," International Review
of Psychiatry vol. 17 (3) (June 2005): 163.

Jensen, Randi J. and Platoni, Katherine T. "Most Military
Efforts Miss Target on Suicide Preventions," The
National Psychologist (November 21, 2018):
https://nationalpsychologist. com/2018/11/most-
military-efforts-miss-target-on-suicide-
prevention/105185.html.

Jeste, Dilip V. "On the State of Psychiatry," *Current
Psychiatry 19 (12)* (December 19, 2020): 34-36; also
available from: https://www.mdedge.com/

psychiatry/article/232726 /dilip-v-jeste-md-state-
psychiatry/page/0/2.

Josephus, Flavius. quoted by the editors, "Masada,"
History (March 4, 2019): https://www.history.com/
topics/ancient-middle-east/masada.

Large, Matthew M. and Ryan, Christopher J. "Disturbing
Findings about the Risk of Suicide and Psychiatric
Hospitals," *Journal of Social Psychiatry and
Psychiatric Epidemiology* vol. 49 (June 2014): 1353-
55; DOI: 10.1007/s00127-014-0912-2.

Leo, J. "Could Suicide Be Contagious?" *Time Magazine*
(February 1986): 59.

Martin, Laura. "Demand for Suicide Prevention Increases,"
Psychiatric Times Online (September 16, 2020):
https://www. psychiatrictimes.com/view/demand-
for-suicide-prevention-increases?utm_source=
sfmc%E2%80%8B&utm_medium=email%E2%80%8
B&utm_campaign=09252020_PT_JAN-20-
PSD0031_TRC_Spravato%E2%80%8B%E2%80%8B&
eKey=31158D64-F01A-4DEA-AC1A-D3CE843FC9BC.

Miller, Greg. "Three Suicide Prevention Strategies Show
Real Promise. How Can They Reach More People?"
Science Magazine (August 22, 2019): https://www.
sciencemag.org/news/2019/08/ three-suicide-
prevention-strategies-show-real-promise-how-can-
they-reach-more-people.

Minot, Paul. "About Me," *Straight Talk Psychiatry* (December 31, 2019): https://paulminotmd.com/about-me/.

Oppenheim, Maya. "Jordan Peterson suffers year of 'absolute hell' and needs emergency treatment for drug addiction that forced him to withdrawal from public life, daughter says," *The Independent* (February 8, 2020): https://www.independent.co.uk/news/world/europe/jordan-peterson-drug-addiction-benzo-valium-xanex-russia-mikhaila-a9324871.html.

Oquendo, Maria A. and Baca-Garcia, Enrique. "Suicidal behavior disorder as a diagnostic entity in the DSM-5 classification system: advantages outweigh limitations," *World Psychiatry: official journal of the World Psychiatric Association (WPA)* vol. 13 (2) (2014): 128-30. doi:10.1002/wps.20116.

Polyakova Maria, Persson, Petra, Hofmann, Katfa, B. Jena Anupam, and Newhouse, Ruth L. "Does Medicine Run in the Family—evidence from three generations of physicians in Sweden: retrospective observational study," *BJM* 371 (December 16, 2020): https://doi.org/10.1136/bmj.m4453.

Piel, Jennifer. "Suicide Risk Following Criminal Arrest," *Psychiatric Times* (December 30, 2020): https://www.psychiatric times.com/view/suicide-risk-following-criminal-arrest?utm_source=sfmc&

utm_medium=email&utm_campaign=01_05_21_P
T_RegScheNL_Recruitment&eKey=ZHJiZXJnZXIuZHJ
AZ21haWwuY29t.

Ramsey, Drew and Oldham, John M. "A Brief History of
American Psychiatry: From a Founding Father to
Dr. Anonymous," *Medscape Psychiatry* (November
7, 2019): https://www.medscape.com/viewarticle/
917451?nlid=132561_424&src=WNL_mdplsfeat_
191112 _mscpedit_psyc&uac=264124BV&spon=
12&impID=2164621&faf=1.

Rush, Benjamin. *An Inquiry into the Influence of Physical
Causes on the Moral Faculty*. February, 1786.

Scardera, Sara, Perret, Lea C., Ouellet-Morin, Isabella, et
al. "Association of Social Support During
Adolescence with Depression, Anxiety, and Suicidal
Ideation in Young Adults," *JAMA Psychiatry*
(December 4, 2020): doi:10.1001/jamanet
workopen.2020.27491.

Seck, Hope Hodge. "This Squad PTSD Therapy Runs Just 2
Weeks. And It's Changing Vet's Lives," *Military*
(November 14, 2019): https://www.military.com/
daily-news/2019/11/14/ squad-style-ptsd-therapy-
runs-just-2-weeks-and-its-changing-vets-lives.html.

Simpson, Scott. "Suicide Risk Screening Tool in Emergency
Departments 'Inadequate," *Psychosomatics: The
Journal of Consultation-Liaison Psychiatry*

(September 2020): https://www.clpsychiatry
.org/aclp-news/y2020/m09/dlin-fischer/.

Spielmans, Glen I., Spence-Sing, Tess, and Parry, Peter
edited by Michael P. Hengartner, Maurizio Pompili,
and Sami Timimi, "Duty to Warn: Antidepressant
Black Box Suicidality Warning is Empirically
Justified," *Frontiers in Psychiatry* (February 13,
2020): https://doi.org/10.3389/fpsyt.2020. 00018.

Swartz, Matthew S. "Teen Suicide Spiked After Debut of
Netflix's '13 Reasons Why,' Study Says," *NPR
Mental Health* (April 30, 2019): https://www.npr.
org/2019/04/30/718529255/teen-suicide-spiked-
after-debut-of-netflixs-13-reasons-why-report-
says.

Tasman, Allan. "The Wrong Way on a Long and Winding
Road: Suicide in the US," *Psychiatric Times Online*,
February 20, 2018, http://www.psychiatric
times.com/couch-crisis/wrong-way-long-and-
winding-road-suicide-us.

Tekin, Serife. "Self and Mental Disorder: Lessons for
Psychiatry from Naturalistic Philosophy,"
Philosophy Compass (Wiley Online Library)
(October 27, 2020: https://doi.org/10.1111/
phc3.12715.

The stories of Ken Hines and Ken Baldwin, "Second
Changes: 'I survived jumping off the Golden Gate

Bridge," *ABC 7 News* (May 18, 2017):
https://abc7news.com/society/second-chances-i-survived-jumping-off-the-golden-gate-bridge/2010562/.

Timimi, Sami. "Insane Medicine: How the Mental Health
    Industry Creates Damaging Treatment Traps and
    How you Can Escape Them," *Mad in America*
    (October 12, 2020): https://www.madinamerica.
    com/2020/10/insane-medicine-preface/.

Van der Jagty-Jelsma, W. de Vries-Schot, M., Scheepers, P.,
    van Deurzen, Pam, Klip, H., and Buitelaar, J.K.
    "Longitudinal Study of Religiosity and Mental
    Health of Adolescents with Psychiatric Problems.
    The TRAILS Study," *The Journal of European
    Psychiatry* vol. 45 (September 2017): 65-71; doi:
    10.1016/j.eurpsy.2017.05.031.

Wolf, Chelsea, Rylander, Melanie, Al-Tayyib, Alia, and
    Simpson, Scott. "After COVID-19 and Beyond the
    Opioid Wave," *Psychiatric Times* (December 29,
    2020): https://www.psychiatrictimes.com/view/
    covid-19-beyond-opioid-wave?utm_source=sfmc
    &utm_medium=email&utm_campaign=01_05_21_
    PT_RegScheNL_Recruitment&eKey=ZHJiZXJnZXIuZ
    HJAZ21haWwuY29t.

Yasgur, Batya Swift. "Three Factors Tied to Higher Suicide
    Risk in Borderline Personality Disorder," *Medscape
    Psychiatry* (November 27, 2020): https://www.

medscape.com/viewarticle/941686?nlid=138509_
424&src=WNL_mdplsfeat_201201_mscpedit_psyc
&uac=264124BV&spon=12&impID=2710242&faf=1
#vp_2.

Zai, Clement C., De Luca, Vincenzo, Strauss, John, Tong,
Ryan P., Sakinofsky, Isaac, and Kennedy, James L.
"Genetic Factors and Suicidal Behavior," *The
Neurobiological Basis of Suicide* edited by Dwivedi
Y, editor (Boca Raton, FL: CRC Press/Taylor &
Francis, 2012), Chapter 11. Available from:
https://www.ncbi.nlm.nih.gov/books/NBK107191/.

Made in the USA
Monee, IL
04 November 2021